THE TRUTH ABOUT
MARIJUANA

THE TRUTH ABOUT MARIJUANA

The American Snake Oil

RAY MARTINEZ

Library of Congress Control Number:		2012907840
ISBN:	Hardcover	978-1-4771-0533-7
	Softcover	978-1-4771-0532-0
	Ebook	978-1-4771-0534-4

For information, please contact Ray Martinez, or R. M. Consulting, Inc., 4121 Stoneridge Court, Fort Collins, CO 80525, or visit www.raymartinez.com.

Although the author and publisher have made every effort to ensure the accuracy and completeness of information contained in this book, we assume no responsibility for errors, inaccuracies, omissions, or any inconsistency herein. Any slights of people, places, or organizations are unintentional.

This book was printed in the United States of America.

To order additional copies of this book, contact:
Xlibris Corporation
1-888-795-4274
www.Xlibris.com
Orders@Xlibris.com
114531

CONTENTS

FOREWORD

Ray's book is a breath of fresh air, clearing the fog of misinformation in much of what you hear about marijuana. As citizens of Fort Collins, my wife and I heard medical marijuana stores were opening and hoped they wouldn't cause drug problems. We have grandkids, and we didn't want them to think our society promotes drug use. Then our worst fears were realized. The stores opened with names claiming that marijuana is organic, herbal, and all about health and wellness. That it is nature's medicine. It was plastered on their storefronts for all our community's youth to see. The marijuana store owners just didn't care. They wanted more customers, and with twenty-one stores competing—more marijuana stores than coffee shops—they would do or say whatever necessary to sell their product. Some of our Fort Collins youth concluded marijuana was safe, and drug violations in the schools shot up three times what they were before the dispensaries opened. There were ten times more drug violations in Colorado Springs.

Ray's book provides the facts that counter the incessant barrage of marijuana propaganda being distributed by one of the largest lobbyists in Washington DC (Marijuana Policy Project). It is a must-read for educators, family therapists, and families. It is especially important reading for families who are in marijuana-battleground areas. Remember, in these areas, the proponents are well funded, have everything to gain financially, and will make arguments that, on the surface, can sound convincing. Ray's book will debunk these myths, arming you with the information you need to prevent attacks on your family's true health and wellness. Ray began his career working to keep Fort Collins safe; and this, his latest book, continues that tradition.

James Patella
Community advocate
Concerned Citizens for Fort Collins Board of Directors

How drug dealers are caught

Special city police team fights war on drugs

It's just before 9 p.m. and six narcotics agents are huddled in the basement of the Fort Collins Police Department getting ready to make a bust.

One of the investigators has been to the house near LaPorte that they will search. He gives his colleagues the lowdown:

He shown each officer which door he will go in and what room he will be responsible for once they are inside. But it's the safety of the innocent family members he's most worried about.

When the officers go in, they must be ready to shoot.

"Keep in mind there are kids, dogs and guns," the investigator says, taking a sip of industrial strength coffee from his filthy mug.

This is common for the Fort Collins Police Special Investigations Unit, a team of nine officers formed to stop drug trafficking. The officers execute a handful of search warrants every month. As on this recent night, what they come up with depends on planning and luck.

By 9:08 the unit is heading out the door — ready to execute a search warrant on a house of a suspected drug dealer.

"OK," reminds team leader Sgt. Raul Martinez, "everybody be careful."

The house is one where confidential informants — CIs — have previously purchased drugs, mostly cocaine.

Martinez says the dealer is

BRIEFING: Members of the Fort Collins Police Special Investigations Unit plan a drug bust.

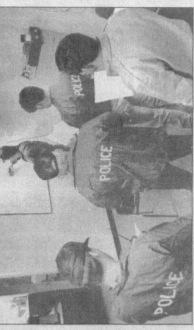

selling to kids who supply local schools.

This is the last night the team can use the search warrant. They had hoped to get word that the dealer would be holding a large quantity of dope within the 10 days after they had the warrant signed by a judge.

Word never came, so on this 10th they they will take whatever they get.

This game of catching the bad guy is one of hit and miss, Martinez says.

"We may go in and get something, we may not. You never can tell until you get there," he

says, turning off the car's lights and coasting in front of the house to see if anyone is home. There it is. That's our car.

He drives to a nearby parking lot where the rest of the team is waiting.

At 9:20 Martinez is sneaking through the back yard of the

house while other officers go to the front door. A barking dog runs up to Martinez.

The cop tells the dog to beat it and the dog runs to the front yard to bark at the other narcs.

When a man answers the door, the cops act fast. They storm the house to ensure nobody destroys evidence.

When the man's wife hears the officers identify themselves at the front door, she stuffs a pipe and some marijuana into the seat cushion where she sits watching TV.

The old trick doesn't fool the narcs.

They check the cushions first and arrest her for possession of marijuana.

During the next three hours, the officers will leave no mattress unturned, no pocket unchecked. They rummage through everything.

The father's *Playboy* and *Penthouse* magazines hidden in the back of the closet, the container of pot stashed in the underwear drawer and every inch of the kids' rooms are checked.

They find a gun, ammunition and $90 in the bedroom.

Stuffed inside a cowboy boot are 20 neatly folded bindles — pages of magazines cut and folded to hold cocaine.

The husband is arrested for a previous drug sale to a confidential informant, and by 11:28 the children return from a friend's house to find nobody home but

the narcs.

As an investigator stands at the front door, keeping the children out of their home, he explains their parents' situation. The kids start crying in the driveway.

While the investigators at the house try to find a place for the children to spend the night, another officer is back at the police station trying to squeeze their father for information.

It's the typical deal: If he helps the narcs bust his own supplier, they will let him off easy.

At 12:18 a.m. the team is back in the basement. A new pot of coffee is brewing. So is a deal.

The coffee will run out before the deal comes through.

It's either too late to find a busy drug dealer on a Saturday night, or the father who is going to jail is lying.

Either way, it's largely a strikeout for the Fort Collins drug team. But the narcs don't mind. They love making life hell for drug dealers.

"We're telling these drug dealers. 'Here's your eviction notice,'" Martinez says with a grin. "We're not going to put up with this."

He says the only way to get drugs out of Fort Collins is to demand action.

"As a unit we believe in zero tolerance," Martinez says. "It doesn't matter if you're snorting a line or dealing a lot, we won't have it."

Fort Collins Police Special Investigations Unit prepare for drug raid March 26, 1989

Permission granted by the *Coloradoan News*; newspaper clipping dated March 26, 1989

PREFACE

I became involved with Concerned Citizens for Fort Collins (CCFC), not because it was popular to do, but because I have worked diligently to enforce and educate people about substance abuse since 1973, when I was an undercover drug agent for Colorado. The CCFC is an ad hoc group who found one another because of our concern about the damaging impact of medical marijuana dispensaries (MMD) industry on our youth, our safety, and the future of our city. We are not affiliated with or sponsored by any group or organization.

Ray Martinez, undercover 1973

There are people who are misled about the genuine use of marijuana for medicinal use. The e-mails and one-on-one discussion that I receive are astounding when I try to narrow down the facts. People who are using the drug for legitimate reasons are much sounder in their reasoning and belief that it is helping them. Whether the drug is acting as a placebo for them or not, most of us really don't know. However, the abusers' reasoning becomes irrational and very vague. If you remember the movie *The Big Lebowski*, when the Dude was questioned if he delivered the money or not, his rationale changed with a lot of ambiguity, and his response was, "Well, there are a lot of ins and outs and what have yous."

Many people will take a person to task with studies that may contradict each other. Well, let's think about that for a moment. Would you fly on an airline if half the pilots told you that the plane was unsafe?

During my time working as an undercover drug agent, narcotics detective, then as a sergeant for the Special Investigations Unit (SIU) (also a drug enforcement unit), I don't ever recall investigating a drug case, regardless of the type of drug, where marijuana was not involved; and I retired from law enforcement after twenty-five years of seeing people destroyed by its abuse and addiction. Unquestionably, alcohol has its toll as well as many other sorts of habits and crimes. What I want to avoid is giving the stamp of approval to another substance that will cost society even more.

**Drug raid in Rifle, CO; marijuana, other drugs,
and paraphernalia was wrapped up inside a U.S. Flag**

—photographed by Ray Martinez

In 1977, another detective and I executed a court-ordered search warrant for a business that was selling drug paraphernalia. We seized it under a court order and were eventually sued for two million dollars in U.S. District Court. After the jury was empanelled and I testified, the judge was incensed, and I could tell the jury members were not pleased with the frivolous law suit either. Consequently, the two attorneys who filed suit settled for a couple of thousand dollars with the first offer from the deputy city attorney; they literally jumped at the offer, saying, "We'll take it!"

The Rand Corporation used to be reputable for their research. However, on September 21, 2011, they made a headline press release that states, "Crime Rises When Medical Marijuana Dispensaries Close." The promarijuana folks use this study as proof why they need the medical marijuana dispensaries (MMDs). The study was heavily debunked for its inaccuracy. What made the study worse or more invalid was that it was only done for twenty-one days after a few stores closed.

UCLA researcher Bridget Freisthler, who is studying crime around dispensaries in Sacramento, criticized the RAND study as "deeply flawed . . ."

The California Police Chiefs Association is at odds with this skimpy research done by the Rand Corporation. The organization's Task Force on Marijuana Dispensaries wrote a 2009 white paper that argued the following, in a section called Ancillary Crimes:

"Throughout California, many violent crimes have been committed that can be traced to the proliferation of marijuana dispensaries. These include armed robberies and murders. For example, as far back as 2002, two home occupants were shot in Willits, California, in the course of a home-invasion robbery targeting medical marijuana. And a series of four armed robberies of a marijuana dispensary in Santa Barbara, California, occurred through August 10, 2006, in which thirty dollars and fifteen baggies filled with marijuana on display were taken by force and removed from the premises in the latest holdup. The owner said he failed to report the first three robberies because "medical marijuana is such a controversial issue."

There was a point and time where our society used to believe that cigarettes were safe and harmless, and some of the tobacco industry led us to believe it was healthy for us to smoke. Sounds familiar with marijuana today? Many years ago, people would sell bottles of drinks that were supposed to cure everything, better known as snake oil. Today we are faced with the twenty-first-century "snake oil" that proponents want you to believe that marijuana cures everything from minor pains to curing cancer. Snake oil never lives up to the sellers' hype. In the old days, they would even use oils from snakes. This term, *snake oil*, was a common phrase used by people years ago, and even today, to refer to products that don't really promote healing in the long run. In the recent show on National Geographic called *American Weed*, aired March 28, 2012, one of the marijuana store owners was promoting his product that was described as "cannabis-infused topical spray intended to help relieve pain" and was labeled "snake oil;" how ironic that the label matches today's science that proves the point that marijuana does not live up to the sellers' hype.

Unfortunately, National Geographic did not live up to its perceived reputation with this program called *American Weed*. I've always believed their programs were documentaries with a balanced approach when it came to science and theories. The *American Weed* program turned out as trying to mimic a reality show promoting the marijuana stores, how to grow, sell, and use marijuana. They even demonstrated how the Stanley brothers made hashish, which, in Colorado, is a felonious crime.

My intention is to bring out the truth about marijuana. Let's be honest, we cannot afford another burden on society with additional healthcare cost because of the health hazards of marijuana, the enforcement, and the ongoing regulatory process of modifying and adding new laws because of the changing times. Even though I think there are people who really need marijuana for medicinal purposes, most people use it as a recreational drug and as a social lubricant. There must be a gatekeeper of all medicines. We shouldn't allow doctors to write notes or prescriptions for medicine that is not approved by the Food and Drug Administration (FDA) and sold through a pharmacy; the FDA is our existing gatekeeper. The pressure to ask doctors to issue permits or notes for their patients to use marijuana because it was approved by a popular vote in Colorado is egregious and unprecedented.

Preface Endnotes

1. News Fix, posted by Jon Brooks, RAND Study: LA Crime Increased When Pot Dispensaries Closed; City Attorney Says Data 'Deeply Flawed', ***http://blogs.kqed.org/newsfix/2011/09/21/rand-study-la-crime-increased-when-pot-dispensaries-close-city-attorney-says-data-deeply-flawed/***, accessed March 16, 2012

2. StopTheDrugWar.com, No evidence Medical Marijuana Dispensaries Cause Crime, RAND Study finds, by Philip Smith, October 3, 2011 (issue #703), *http://stopthedrugwar.org/chronicle/2011/oct/03/no_evidence_medical_marijuana_di,* accessed March 16, 2012

ACKNOWLEDGEMENTS

Director Thomas J. Gorman, Rocky Mountain High Intensity
Drug Trafficking Area

Scoot Crandall, Director of Team Fort Collins

Nancy Patella, Community Advocate

Bob Powell, Character First

Josh Ritter, Deputy District Attorney,
Eighth Judicial District, Colorado

Jean Troxell, Executive Assistant for the Center for Family Care

Mike Demma, Team Fort Collins

Ron Maulsby, Retired Poudre School District Principal
and Assistant Superintendent

Darcie Votipka, Poudre School District

Jerry Wilson, PhD, Poudre School District Superintendent

Ray Romero, Graphic Artist

Don Butler, Business Owner

Ray Jackson, Pittsburg Steelers Football Team

Jim Kyle, Former Colorado Undercover Drug Agent

The Society for the Prevention of Drug-Pushing Profits

"The loss of one youth's potential is a tragic loss to that individual, his family, and the community at large, and as you know, those lost souls often become a never-ending burden to those that love them and society as a whole . . . National Geographic has given so much airtime and sympathy to the marijuana folks, limiting you to sound bites, omitting the many times you would have told them the impact on our youth . . . I am so glad you are writing the book and doing so in such a short amount of time."

Nancy Smith, PhD
Therapist in Fort Collins, Colorado
Licensed Professional Counselor (LPC) in Colorado
Founding Director of the Center for Family Care,
Ft. Collins, Colorado

"Ray should be commended for exposing the dangers and myths surrounding marijuana. The forces pushing for states to legalize medical marijuana are hiding their true agenda. Marijuana is a cash crop to these organized criminal forces. Their concern is not for their fellow man but for their bottom line. It is ironic that the rampant abuses on medical marijuana laws only serve to make our communities and society sick and less productive."

Cliff Riedel
Career Prosecutor
Assistant District Attorney, Eighth Judicial District of Colorado

"Policy discussions have to be made by weighing the benefits against the cost to the citizens. Let your city council representatives know how you want them to handle the commercial distribution of marijuana in your community . . . Marijuana use among our children has led directly to Poudre School District suspensions that have tripled over the last couple years. We also know that police are reporting an increase in home invasions and criminal activity that has a direct relationship to the availability of marijuana. Further, students are reporting that they often obtain access to marijuana through relatives and friends who have medical marijuana permits. And we know that dispensaries are a clear violation of the federal Controlled Substance Act . . ."

Larry Abrahamson
District Attorney, Eighth Judicial District of Colorado

"Experience taught me twenty years ago that drugs and alcohol are involved in the vast majority of incidents that are called into us. However, the prevalence of marijuana as a significant factor seemed to be going through the roof. Routinely, deputies noted that DUI arrests involved drivers smoking pot; deputies came across illegal possession of user amounts of pot where the suspect stated it was for medical purposes but did not have a state card; citizens reported illegal pot grows in their neighborhoods; we experienced home-invasion robberies into pot grows or pot dealers' homes, people reported being kidnapped and later admitted the "kidnappings" were actually drug rip offs, and kids were getting caught possessing pot at schools. The list just went on and on."

Justin Smith
Sheriff, Larimer County, CO

"Ray candidly brings to light the dangers and adverse effects of the use of marijuana and the abuses committed by medical marijuana distribution facilities. This book should be mandatory reading for our elected representatives who make decisions relating to proposals for legalization of marijuana and/or the creation of medical marijuana outlets."

Stu VanMeveren
Former Elected District Attorney and Criminal Defense Attorney

"Ray is a gifted writer who has authored many superb self-help and inspirational books. Ray's new book thoroughly unmasks the medical marijuana myth. Ray points out that the idea of medical marijuana is a mirage. It is not prescribed by the family physician, but by typical pill-pushing doctors traveling the circuit. It is not dispensed by licensed pharmacies. It is about drug pushers selling marijuana for profit. It is about marijuana abusers getting stoned. It is about stoned drivers causing carnage on the highways. It is about ruined lives. You will find this to be a useful reference book."

Loren Schall
Former Deputy, Chief Trial Deputy,
and Assistant District Attorney (1970-2009),
Eighth Judicial District of Colorado (Larimer and Jackson Counties)

"Many employers provide health insurance, and yet this "medicine" and the doctors who prescribe the vast majority are not recognized under any health-benefit plan. The MMD industry has taken an effective caregiver model and created a recreational use demand that has employers very concerned. The rate of growth of young men between the ages of twenty-four and forty obtaining medical marijuana licenses for "chronic pain" is a red flag to employers."

Carl Maxey
*Business Owner in Fort Collins,
CO-Worked in the manufacturing, distribution, and trucking industries*

"More than seventy-five Colorado communities have already closed MMDs with no reports of lack of access to marijuana from a caregiver or increases in neighborhood crime. Let's be honest and stand up for what's best for our community. Under Amendment 20, voter intent did not allow for retail distribution on marijuana. MMDs have brought increased crime in Fort Collins with marijuana being noted in law-enforcement reports as compared to data before MMDs were established in Fort Collins in 2008."

Wade Troxell, PhD
*City Council Member, Fort Collins, Colorado,
Professor at Colorado State University*

DRUG CACHE: A police officer checks some of the 33 pot plants found in a home in south-central Fort Collins.

Police seize pot plants

Tip leads special unit
to raid home, arrest 1

By KEVIN VAUGHAN
The Coloradoan

Police officers armed with a search warrant arrested a 29-year-old man Thursday night and confiscated 33 marijuana plants.

Kevin T. Starr was taken into custody about 8:30 p.m. after seven members of a city-county drug unit kicked in the door of his home at 2821 Eagle Drive in south-central Fort Collins.

"This isn't for personal use," Fort Collins police Sgt. Ray Martinez said as he surveyed an upstairs bedroom where 33 pot plants were found. "In my opinion, this is cultivation for distribution."

Starr was booked into the Larimer County Detention Center for investigation of growing marijuana with the intent of selling it.

Cultivation of marijuana is a felony. Starr is scheduled to appear in court at 1:30 p.m. today to be advised of his rights. The district attorney's office will decide what formal charges to file against the man.

Martinez said the pot plants, most of which were at least two feet tall, could produce about a pound of marijuana each. On the street a pound is selling for more than $1,000, making the plants

worth a total of at least $33,000, he said. The pot could yield more money if it was broken into smaller quantities.

The police officers and sheriff's deputies had a search warrant when they approached the home about 8:30 p.m.

After announcing they were outside, officers kicked in the door and arrested Starr, clad only in a towel.

Martinez said investigators received an anonymous tip that pot was being grown at the home.

In an upstairs bedroom they found the plants spread across a plastic tarpaulin that covered the floor. A huge growing light hung from the ceiling, and officers found a thermometer, a moisture meter and a humidifier — all signs that the plants were being carefully grown.

In the basement, officers found other drug paraphernalia, including a bong and plastic bags like those used to hold marijuana.

"You've got to hit the cultivators as well as the dealers," said Martinez, head of the police department's Special Investigations Unit. "The message is that we're not going to focus on what the trend or the news item is.

"We're going to focus on what will stop the flow."

BUSTING IN: Officers bust in the house's door to start the drug raid.

Fort Collins Special Investigations Unit
conduct a marijuana home-growing operation in the late 1980s.

CHAPTER 1

Voters Rights about Marijuana Stores

Many of you are aware that a petition was circulated in Fort Collins, Colorado, to ask voters if they want to allow voters to decide as to whether marijuana distribution centers be allowed in the City of Fort Collins or not; this was never voted on before by the people. In fact, it was decided, in 2009, by unelected officials who overturned your vote, thus departing from Colorado's Amendment 20 and allowing storefront marijuana distribution.

In 2000, Colorado voters approved Amendment 20 of the Colorado Constitution to allow medical marijuana use. The amendment doesn't allow distribution through dispensaries. Since that decision, parents, schools, substance-abuse treatment providers, and police officials have experienced significant negative effects plaguing our youth and our community.

The decision to allow or deny these dispensaries represents a significant public-policy issue for any community. The voters deserve the opportunity to vote as to whether they want to allow these marijuana distribution centers in their community.

The June 26, 2011, *Coloradoan News* quote—"'Banning medical marijuana centers would deprive patients of the medicine and professional guidance they need to treat ailments such as chronic pain and muscle spasms,' said Terri Gomez, campaign manager for the group,"—is misleading. Colorado was the only state that allowed solely commercialized marijuana. All other states are functioning very well with providing marijuana to people who truly need it without the commercialized stores. The 'professional guidance' is given by doctors, not marijuana store clerks.

Under the law, patients are allowed one primary caregiver. The absence of regulatory practices has resulted in some "patients" registering with numerous caregivers, allowing them to purchase more marijuana than recommended by the intended primary caregiver. This has created an abundant supply of marijuana for sale in what is now known as the new black market.

On April 26, 2011, the U.S. attorney for Colorado reversed course in a memo to the Colorado attorney general advising state officials that they will not condone distribution of marijuana in the state and will federally prosecute because of the growing problems. Why is the city council acting in defiance of the law, when they were sworn into office to uphold the law? The Fort Collins City Council approved some of the most lax regulations in the state on the marijuana shops (overriding almost all restrictions on proximity to schools, daycare centers, etc.).

Local law-enforcement officials are seeing an increase in violent or dangerous crimes relating to marijuana usage since the decriminalization of these commercial distributors, while at the same time, other crimes are generally falling, and overall public-safety budgets are decreasing for many law-enforcement agencies.

Now more than ever is the time for our elected officials to act, and if they cannot, then let the voters decide.

CHAPTER 2

Comparing Apples to Oranges

Too often we want to compare sacred habits or addictions to other things in life as being far worse. Addiction drives us into reasoning why it is okay. However, the trouble with addiction is that a person doesn't know what they are addicted to until he or she runs out of what they are addicted too. In this case, there is a common thought that marijuana is not any worse than alcohol or that alcohol is worse. Additionally, some people are convinced that there isn't any addiction associated with marijuana.

An interview of Gabriel G. Nahas, MD, PhD, a research professor of anesthesiology at the College of Physicians and Surgeons at Columbia University in New York City, who has written four hundred scientific articles, states that there is an effect on the brain cell. "After a brain cell is stimulated by the chemical contained in marijuana, it will never be exactly the same. It will 'remember'; it will be imprinted with a chemical memory. This imprint in the brain is usually associated with a pleasant feeling, and it is this association which induces the desire to take more. This is what, broadly speaking, is called addiction. People usually limit the word addiction to heroin or opiates, because when the body is deprived of these chemicals, the user will suffer withdrawal symptoms. However, having withdrawal symptoms is only reinforcement to addiction; it's not the whole story."

The *2011 World Drug Report* paints a detailed picture of marijuana abusers. Among cannabis users in treatment in the United States, 80.5 percent are not married, 90 percent have obtained an education of twelve years or less; 25 percent are unemployed, and 46 percent are not in the labor force (of which 55 percent are students). Of the cannabis users who entered treatment services from 2000 to 2008, nearly a quarter report psychiatric problems. In addition, new research suggests that driving under the influence of marijuana could double a person's risk of getting in a serious or fatal car crash.

Why should we promote the legalization of a substance that can irretrievably harm our children's brains and makes our citizens less intelligent, less productive, and less safe? Open and unrestricted drug use cannot coexist with a free, safe, and productive society.

Some people believe too many people are in prison for simple possession of marijuana. The Office of National Drug Control Policy recently reported that of all the inmates in state prisons, *0.3 percent is arrested for offenses involving only marijuana possession.*

According to the Drug Enforcement Administration, seven hundred thousand fewer teenagers used illicit drugs in 2010 than a decade earlier, a 16 percent decline. From 2000 to 2010, current marijuana use by teens has dropped 9 percent, methamphetamine use by teens has plummeted 60 percent, LSD use has dropped 50 percent, and current cocaine use among high school seniors has dropped 38 percent.

There have been other important victories too. In the late 1980s and early 1990s, with the help of the Partnership for a Drug-Free America, America's policymakers and opinion shapers got tough on drugs. Through movies, television, mass media, and, yes, sermons, America sent a message: Drug use is not culturally or morally acceptable, and it will not be tolerated. The nation was committed to defeating the cocaine epidemic, and it did.

We have much work left in our own fight against drugs. We need more drug education and prevention classes in schools, more rehabilitation and treatment centers, and more resources for law-enforcement officials. But all this is for naught if our nation's leaders, including its religious leaders, undermine and abandon the cause.

During a recent trip to Mexico, Vice President Joe Biden was right to reject the idea of legalization. "There is no possibility the Obama-Biden administration will change its policy on legalization," he said. It's time for a new bipartisan coalition committed to defending our children and our future from the dangers of drug abuse and addiction.

Chapter 2 Endnotes

1. *2011 World Drug Report, http://www.unodc.org/documents/data-and-analysis/WDR2011/World_Drug_Report_2011_ebook.pdf*, accessed March 15, 2012

2. U.S. News Health, Pot Use Could Double Risk of Car Crash, Research Shows, By Steven Reinberg, *HealthDay Reporter, http://health.usnews.com/health-news/news/articles/2012/02/10/pot-use-could-double-risk-of-car-crash-research-shows*, accessed March 15, 2012

3. MARIJUANA: The greatest cause of illegal drug abuse, Office of National Drug Control Policy Executive Office of the President Washington, DC 20503 July 2008, *http://www.justice.gov/dea/statistics/Marijuana_2008.pdf*, accessed March 15, 2012

4. U.S. Drug Enforcement Administration, *http://www.justice.gov/dea/2010_successes.html*, accessed March 15, 2012

5. William J. Bennett, a CNN contributor, is the author of *The Book of Man: Readings on the Path to Manhood.* He was U.S. secretary of education from 1985 to 1988 and director of the Office of National Drug Control Policy under President George H.W. Bush, *http://www.thomasnelson.com/the-book-of-man.html*

6. Gabriel G. Nahas, MD, PhD, a research professor of anesthesiology at the College of Physicians and Surgeons at Columbia University in New York City, who has written four hundred scientific articles, interview by LISTEN, Journal of Better Living.

CHAPTER 3

The Myths of Drug Legalization

I am deeply impressed with Thomas J. Gorman's, director of the Rocky Mountain High-Intensity Drug-Trafficking Area, passion and intensive research and analysis about the mythical statements made by those who favor legalization of marijuana or drugs in general. You will find that the information you are about to read in this chapter is a breath of fresh air when it comes to the truth, but on the other hand, the facts demonstrates the trouble we are in and how blinded people are with misinformation. Tom Gorman was the former deputy chief of the California Attorney General's Bureau of Narcotic Enforcement (BNE). He has served as an undercover agent and narcotics investigator, served as a program manager for the Attorney General's Advanced Training Center in Sacramento, headed the Sacramento County Heroin Impact Program and the State Department of Justice Special Investigations Organized Crime Unit.

Just as in the 1970s, the drug legalization movement has received a great deal of media attention. Also, as in the 1970s, this movement, unfortunately, has contributed to the rise in drug use by painting the picture that drug laws—not drugs—are the villains. Legalization advocates attempt to support their position with faulty analogies, misrepresentations, and unsupported theories.

One example I often hear about is that the marijuana plant was given by God for us to use. Well, so were the coca and opiate plants, but I am finding it difficult to believe that God wanted us to abuse them by developing heroin or cocaine to snort for recreation. The peyote cactus is not intended for us to extract mescaline for hallucinating abuse. The psilocybin mushroom, another hallucinogenic substance, also referred to as God's flesh, is not intended to use as an abusive high; it is amazing what terminology people use to make the drug abuse sound fun and morally correct to abuse.

The following facts will address the myths propagated by the pro-drug movement.

MYTH: *Drug laws infringe on individual freedom and privacy as well as make criminals out of otherwise law-abiding citizens.*

FACT: All laws, by their nature, restrict a certain degree of freedom—the freedom to do as one pleases, whenever one pleases, regardless of the harm or potential harm to oneself or others. Civilized society has the right and the responsibility to regulate behavior in order to protect individuals from their own poor decisions as well as others from the risks of certain behavior. Drunk driving, traffic regulations, possession of explosives and weapons, incest, and child labor are but a few examples.

Those who want to legalize drugs would have you believe that individuals who choose to engage in illegal behavior bear no responsibility, but instead, the law is to blame, even though most of our citizens elect not to violate the law. The legalization advocates focus on the rights of drug users while ignoring the rights of the public. Based on their philosophy, it is acceptable to allow a very small segment of our society to get high with impunity while placing the majority in great jeopardy from their intoxicated state. Based on their theory, drunk driving should not be against the law. A drunk should only be punished after he or she has a traffic accident and kills or maims someone.

Additionally, the majority of our citizens do not fear law enforcement. It is those few who choose to violate the law who feel threatened by the police. They seek protection of their own freedom while they choose to violate the freedom of others.

MYTH: *Drug use is a victimless crime.*

FACT: There are actually four classes of drug-use victims: the users themselves, the family and friends of users, the individuals who are victimized by the acts of those under the influence, and the taxpayers/consumers who are paying the price. Tell these people, who have had firsthand experience with drug abusers, that they are not victims. Tell the mother and father whose child was killed by a drugged driver or the husband whose wife was raped by somebody loaded on cocaine or the sister whose brother was brutally beaten by a speed freak that they are not victims of drug use. The nexus between violence and being under the influence is indisputable. Tragic stories of promising young adults dropping out or children beaten by their drug-using parents are all too common. How anyone, assuming that they truly understand the drug culture, can suggest a policy that would facilitate drug use is beyond comprehension.

MYTH: *Alcohol and illicit drugs are no different; thus, it is hypocritical for society to allow alcohol use while outlawing other drugs.*

FACT: Alcohol and illicit drugs have a major difference. Most people use alcohol as a beverage and don't drink to become intoxicated; whereas, with drugs, intoxication is the sole purpose. That is why marijuana smokers seek the higher THC content in marijuana and why crack is so popular among cocaine users. A more factual analogy would be to compare drug use with drunkenness. In addition, illicit drugs are far more addicting than alcohol. Also, approximately one-half of our citizens use alcohol, whereas only approximately 8 percent use illicit drugs. In fact, there are almost as many people addicted to alcohol as use illicit drugs. The reason is that alcohol is legal, relatively inexpensive, readily available, and socially acceptable, whereas illicit drugs are not.

MYTH: *The legalization of illicit drugs should be based on the alcohol model.*

FACT: Alcohol is hardly the model to use to justify legalizing illicit drugs. Legal alcohol has been consumed by a majority of our young people, whereas only a small percentage uses illegal drugs.

There are almost as many people addicted to alcohol than use all the illicit drugs combined. Alcohol kills five times more people, the medical costs are triple, and economic costs are double those of all illicit drugs combined. There are also three times as many arrests for alcohol offenses as there are for drug offenses. The paradox is, while society is strengthening and demanding stricter enforcement of alcohol laws, there are those who want to decriminalize and even abolish drug laws.

MYTH: *We tried alcohol prohibition, which was a failure, proving that prohibition against drugs does not work.*

FACT: Alcohol prohibition, under quite different circumstances in the 1920s, was an attempt to pass laws that the majority of the people did not support. Even with that, there was an approximate 50 percent reduction in alcohol consumption, deaths from alcohol-related diseases, admissions to mental institutions, and alcohol-related psychosis. Unlike the legalizers would lead you to believe, crime did not skyrocket. Prior to enforcing drug laws and alcohol prohibition from 1900 to 1920, the murder rate jumped 300 percent (1.5 to 8 per 100,000). During prohibition, the rate climbed only 30 percent (8 to 9.5 per 100,000). Rescinding prohibition after only thirteen years was insufficient time to change society's attitude following two thousand years of acceptance. Regardless of whether you drink alcohol or not, you would probably agree that our society would be much better off if we did not have alcoholic beverages.

MYTH: *Elimination of drugs would reduce crime and free prison space for the more serious violent offenders.*

FACT: Removal of laws would reduce incidents for those specific violations, but the behavior would not change. Lowering the age of consent to twelve would reduce the number of child molestation crimes, but it would not change the fact that predators were molesting young children ages twelve to eighteen. The advocates fail to recognize what drug experts are well aware of—that a high percentage of drug dealers were criminals first. They would continue their criminal behavior in order to acquire sources of income. The Mafia did not disband after prohibition, nor would the Crips and

Bloods become choirboys if drugs were legalized. The drug black market would continue unless all drugs for all ages were legalized, a proposal few support.

The nexus between being under the influence of alcohol and/or drugs and violence is well documented. Because drugs alter the mental state, drug users commit a disproportionate number of violent crimes. These acts of violence are often against family members and friends. Fifty percent of all child abuse cases are attributed to drug-using parents. Drug users are five to ten times more likely to be involved in fatal traffic accidents than drunk drivers. The perpetrator was under the influence in well over half of the violent crimes such as murder, rape, and serious assault. Only 5 percent of all murders are committed because of drug laws, whereas approximately 25 percent are committed because the murderer was under the influence of drugs.

There are three times as many arrests for alcohol violations as there are for drug violations. Legalizing substances such as alcohol was supposed to reduce crime, or is it that intoxication leads to more crime?

Ninety-three percent of all state-prison inmates are violent and/or serious repeat offenders. Only 1.4 percent are first time, "nonviolent" drug offenders. Keep in mind that "non-violent" only describes the act for which individuals are incarcerated and not their history or previous behavior. If an organized-crime hit man were convicted for income tax evasion, then he would be considered a nonviolent inmate. In addition, only approximately 10 percent of those arrested for drug offenses actually end up in prison. The simple truth is that if we legalize or decriminalize drugs, the acts of violence against our citizens would skyrocket.

MYTH: *Other countries have had successful experience with a more lenient and/or pseudolegalized drug policy.*

FACT: In the 1970s, legalization advocates cited Great Britain's decriminalization of heroin as a model drug policy. When Britain's failed policy resulted in increased addiction, while the addict population remained stable in the United States, the advocates discontinued citing Britain. They then pointed to Platzspitz Park in Zurich, Switzerland, which essentially offered free drugs. This program was to prove all the so-called positive benefits of legalized drugs. The advocates expected less crime, more addicts accepting treatment, decreased AIDS, and the isolation of addicts. After five years, this experiment was abandoned because crime increased, drug-related deaths doubled, AIDS rose, and the health care system was overwhelmed. The very-persistent advocates then began focusing on the Netherlands and its "enlightened" drug policy of not enforcing laws against selling and using marijuana in certain areas. After a number of years, the Netherlands began experiencing the consequences of lenient drug laws with increased drug use, unemployment, and crime. From 1984 to 1992, teenage drug use in the Netherlands increased 250 percent, while in the United States, at the same time, teenage drug use was reduced by 50 percent. Crimes of violence in the Netherlands—for instance, serious assault—increased 65 percent.

The advocates actually don't have to look beyond this country to examine the results of legalization. The experience in Alaska with decriminalized marijuana resulted in twice as many Alaskan teenagers using the drug as those in the rest of the nation. Also, in the early 1900s, prior to legal sanctions, when drugs were inexpensive, available, and legal, the drug crisis per capita was triple today's drug problem.

The advocates failed to examine the assertive drug policies of Japan and Singapore that resulted in the virtual elimination of the drug problem. Along with some Muslim countries, Japan and Singapore have proven that tough drug laws, coupled with aggressive enforcement, work.

There is evidence to show that a zero-tolerance approach to policing is more effective:

The Swedish Government has adopted a tough approach to drugs use based on tough and consistent enforcement of the law and prevention policies. Only 9 percent of Swedes have tried drugs *(1)*, compared with 34 percent of British people ages between sixteen and fifty-nine.*(2)*

The former mayor of New York Rudolph Giuliani has said that he favors arresting anyone caught in possession of cannabis.*(3)* Mayor Giuliani enforced a zero-tolerance policy toward all types of crime, including cannabis possession, from 1994 to 2001. In that time, the number of burglaries and the number of murders in New York both fell by nearly two-thirds.*(4)* Enforcing this policy consistently across all drugs had amazing results. In New York City, crack cocaine is widely considered a thing of the past.*(5)*

1. *The Sunday Times*, 8 July 2001
2. *Drug misuse declared in 2000: results from the British Crime Survey, Op cit*, Table 2.1, page 13
3. *Daily Mail*, 15 February 2002
4. CompStat Citywide Year Historical Comparison 2001 through 1993, Police Department City of New York see *http://www.nyc.gov/html/nypd/html/pct/cspdf.html* as at 8 April 2002
5. *The Herald*, 3 April 2002

MYTH: *The cost of enforcing drug laws is too expensive, and the money could better be spent on social programs dealing with the root causes of drug abuse.*

FACT: What the legalization advocates fail to address is the cost to this country if drug laws were not enforced. Making illicit drugs legal, inexpensive, and readily available would lead to a significant increase in the number of users and increased consumption among current users. Increased use and consumption would result in corresponding greater costs for homelessness, unemployment, welfare, lost productivity, disability payments, school dropouts, lawsuits, medical care, chronic mental illness, accidents, crime, and child neglect, to name a few.

Fifty to sixty percent of mental health care patients are substance abusers. Drug-using teens are three times more likely to commit suicide than their non-using peers. Seventy-five percent of teenage runaways are substance abusers. Hundreds of thousands of newborns are drug exposed and impaired, costing taxpayers over $100,000 per child.

The current economic cost of illicit drug abuse is still half that of one legal drug—alcohol. The money raised in taxing alcohol covers less than 10 percent of all social and health expenditures due to that drug. Federal, state, and local government expenditures for drug law enforcement, which includes police, prosecutors, public defenders, courts, and prisons, are less than 1 percent of total government expenditures. Relatively speaking, this is not a significant investment, considering drug law enforcement, when compared to alcohol, helps save hundreds of thousands of lives and hundreds of billions of dollars.

Putting drug law-enforcement expenditures into perspective, our federal government spent ten times that amount paying the interest on the public debt, ten times that amount on the war on poverty, and more money on the Food Stamp Program alone than all federal, state, and local expenditures for drug law enforcement.

There is also an assumption that with legalization, there would be no governmental costs to regulate and control the distribution, sale, and use of drugs similar to those we currently have with alcohol. In addition, drug law enforcement would still be required for those drugs that remain illegal or to police the sale to and use by those underage.

Most importantly, the cost-saving argument, referred to as blind-side economics, only addresses economic issues and not the more tragic costs in terms of loss of life, pain and suffering, broken families, child neglect, and the general poisoning of Americans.

MYTH: *The answer to the drug problem is increased drug prevention and treatment and not law enforcement.*

FACT: It is interesting to note that most drug treatment and prevention professionals are against legalizing drugs. They consider law enforcement an essential precursor to both successful prevention and treatment. Good drug policy requires all three disciplines.

Drug-treatment experts agree that law enforcement offers strong incentives not only to receive treatment but, once treatment has been completed, to stay off of drugs. Making drugs legal, inexpensive, and readily available would eliminate that important incentive. Drug-prevention experts agree that legal sanctions and public attitude against drug use are essential for successful education and prevention programs.

MYTH: *This country's eighty-year war on drugs has been a failure, proving that strict laws and enforcement do not work.*

FACT: It should be noted that there is not actually a "war" on drugs, but a limited engagement. Even with that, drug sanctions and enforcement have been successful during this eighty-year period. Experts estimate that in the early 1900s, prior to drug laws or enforcement, there were as many addicts in this country as there are today, even though the population was one-third smaller. Recognizing the tremendous costs and problems associated with drug use, citizens, through their government, elected to pass and strictly enforce drug laws. The drug problem was significantly reduced so that by the 1940s and '50s, it was relatively minor. Anyone attending high school during that period could testify that drugs were virtually nonexistent for most people.

In the 1960s and 1970s, there was a major shift in attitude regarding drug use. Terms such as "recreational drug use" were coined, the legalization movement gained momentum, drug use was glorified, and drug law enforcement was deemphasized. This resulted in a tremendous increase in drug use and related problems in America. In the 1980s, through a combination of increased law enforcement, highly publicized prevention messages, and more effective treatment, drug use was reduced by 50 percent in just twelve years. In 1979, there were 24 million drug users, and by 1992, there were only 11.4 million. It was during that period that drug arrests and incarcerations doubled. High school seniors graduating in the class of 1992 were 50 percent less likely to use drugs than their counterparts in the class of 1979.

Studies and surveys show that while 70 percent of eighth graders had used alcohol, only 10 percent had tried marijuana and only 2 percent cocaine. Additional studies demonstrate that a majority of students cite the fear of getting into trouble with the law as a major deterrent to drug use. Yet another study shows that 79 percent of those responding stated they had no chance to use cocaine. Of the 21 percent who did have a chance to use cocaine, over half did. The U.S. military's tough drug policy dropped drug use from 28 percent in 1980 to 3 percent in 1992. Private industry has repeatedly proven that tough antidrug sanctions are successful.

There have been few modern social problems in this country, such as welfare, teenage pregnancy, homelessness, high school dropouts, and test scores for American students that have shown the same degree of success as our country's drug policy. If for instance, teen pregnancies were reduced by 50 percent, homelessness reduced by 50 percent, or SAT scores raised by 50 percent, the successes would be applauded. Instead, a 50 percent reduction in the number of drug users is considered a failure.

Conclusion

You don't have to be a drug-abuse expert, an intellectual, or someone holding a variety of degrees to understand that to make illicit drugs legal, readily available, relatively inexpensive, and reduce the risk would lead to increased numbers of drug users as well as increased consumption among current users. Likewise, common sense would dictate that with increased drug use and consumption, the problems affecting this country would be overwhelming. Drug abuse exacerbates most social problems facing this country and touches all segments of our population. There would be no greater threat to destroy our country from within than making drugs inexpensive, available, and legal. I don't think this is a legacy that we want to leave our children or our grandchildren. Instead of repeating the mistake of the 1970s, we should build on the successes of the 1980s. It is a mystery as to what drug culture the legalization advocates are referencing. Drug-abuse experts are positive it isn't the one they deal with on a daily basis. Intellectual theory, although interesting, often has no basis in reality.

1973 drug bust/purchase of 100 lbs of marijuana
in Boulder, CO. Ray Martinez, on the right,
as undercover drug agent who made the purchase.

CHAPTER 4

Medical Marijuana Distribution Centers
Questions/Answers

Medical Marijuana Centers (Dispensaries) = De Facto Legalization = Increased Use

Q: *What are the primary factors that affect the rate of drug abuse in a community?*

1. **Price.** Generally, higher cost results in less use and lower cost leads to greater use. This is simple economics.
2. **Availability.** The more readily available a substance is, the greater the use; the less readily available the lower the use. This includes 'search time' which is how long it takes to obtain the drug. The longer it takes, the less inclined some are to use.
3. **Perception of Risk.** Risk includes a) getting in trouble and b) physical and psychological dangers. The higher perception of risk results in less use, and the lower perception of risk lead to greater use.
4. **Public Attitude:.** Public includes family units, neighborhoods, communities, states, and nations. The more accepting these public units are of drug use, the greater the use, and the less accepting the lower the use.

Q: *How do these factors relate when comparing the two legal substances, alcohol and cigarettes, with illegal drugs?*

1. **Alcohol.** Alcohol, unlike illicit drugs, is relatively inexpensive and readily available, has low perception of risk, and is publicly acceptable. The results are as follows:

o   Over 130 million people regularly drink alcohol, many to the point of intoxication.[1]

o   There are almost as many people who meet the diagnostic criteria for alcohol abuse or alcoholism (approximately 14 million)1 as have used marijuana within the last thirty days (approximately 15 million).[4]

o   More than half of American adults have a close family member who has or has had alcoholism.[1]

o   Approximately 25 percent of U.S. youth are exposed to alcohol abuse or alcohol dependence in the family.[1]

o   In 2008, an estimated 11,773 people died in alcohol-impaired driving accidents.[6]

2. **Cigarettes.** The same is true for cigarette smoking when in 1965, around 50 percent of our adults regularly smoked cigarettes. That trend is changing. In 2008, approximately 20.6 percent (forty-six million) of U.S. adults were current smokers. Consumption per capita went from 4,259 cigarettes in 1965 to 1,691 in 2006.[3] Why the change?

o   Cigarettes have become much more expensive (¢30 a pack to $5 a pack).

o   Cigarettes are less readily available. The days are gone when there was a cigarette pack in almost every pocket; cigarette vending machines in every lobby and cigarette girls went from table to table.

o   The perception of health risk related to cigarette smoking is extremely high. Also, cigarette smoking is becoming more restrictive (prohibited). There are fewer places an individual can smoke cigarettes. In many regions, hotels, restaurants, bars, public buildings, public transportation, etc. have banned smoking cigarettes. Often, cigarette smokers are forced to go outside, away from a building entrance.

o   Public attitude has changed toward smokers. They are often frowned upon for having that terrible habit and the smell that permeates their clothing.

Note: While attempting to prevent widespread drug abuse, it does not make sense to ease restrictions on marijuana use when cigarette-smoking restrictions are showing such success. Marijuana has not only more adverse physical and psychological effects than tobacco, but it causes intoxication. There is a reason why terms such as *stoned* or *wasted* are common among marijuana users.

Summary:

o   One hundred thirty million regularly drink alcohol (forty million alcohol abuse or alcoholism)

o   Forty-six million regularly smoke cigarettes

o   Approximately fifteen million have smoked a marijuana cigarette within the last thirty days

Q: *How do medical marijuana distribution centers or dispensaries impact general marijuana use?*

There are a number of ways that dispensaries encourage marijuana use. They are the same factors that affect the rate of drug use in a community. Dispensaries are de facto legalization of marijuana.

o   **Availability.** Dispensaries sell a variety of marijuana products openly to anyone with a medical marijuana card, which is easily attainable. Dispensaries are motivated by profit; the more patients, the greater the profit. When dispensaries in Colorado exploded beginning in February 2009, the number of patients soared from a few thousand to an estimate of over a hundred thousand by the end of 2010. Marijuana smokers realize if a person wants to use marijuana with impunity, he/she need only to obtain a card. With a card, a person cannot only legally possess and use marijuana but legally purchase up to the equivalent of 108 cigarettes at a time from dispensaries. As long as there is profit, there will be rogue doctors who will improperly recommend marijuana. Rest assured, the individuals operating dispensaries will know which doctors to refer to potential clients.

o   **Perception of Risk.** Since marijuana is legal both for the dispensary and the user, there is no risk of getting into trouble.

An individual with a card can buy and possess up to two ounces of marijuana at a time. The articles and advertisements by promarijuana proponents profess that marijuana is relatively safe. The fact that the public has called marijuana a medicine fortifies the belief that it is relatively safe, which is the same issue with pharmaceutical drug abuse: "How can a medicine be unsafe to use?" Furthermore, dispensaries have the right to advertise their products. We have already seen dispensary advertising that directly targets young people, who are most vulnerable to the effects of advertising and the ill effects of marijuana.

o **Public Attitude.** Public attitude, or at least the perception of public attitude toward marijuana, has become much more tolerant, particularly with the medical marijuana issue.

Note: Three of the four factors that lead to increased drug use are present with the medical marijuana industry and de facto legalization of marijuana. Society should not be surprised at the future results.

For the first time in a decade, the decline in marijuana use among youth (down 23 percent from 2001 to 2006) has stopped with a slight uptick between 2007 and 2009. Many drug experts cite the medical marijuana movement as affecting teens' attitudes on marijuana.

Q: *But isn't marijuana a relatively harmless drug?*

Any drug that causes intoxication is not harmless. The promarijuana movement plays down, in public, the intoxicating effect of marijuana. In private, many brag about being stoned and the high THC content of marijuana they smoked. The effects of being wasted or stoned are seldom positive on the individual, the individual's family or friends, and on society in general. The effects of marijuana intoxication vary with the individual, just as they do with alcohol.

There are thousands of studies from medical and other legitimate research professionals that have documented the adverse effects of marijuana use. These studies can be found online and at the

University of Mississippi's Research Institute of Pharmaceutical Sciences. These adverse effects include but are not limited to:

- Intoxication
- Reduced coordination
- Distorted perception
- Concentration difficulties
- Impaired learning functions

- Dependence
- Respiratory illness
- Impaired brain development
- Impaired short-term memory
- Greater risk of cancer

These adverse effects, in turn, increase the prevalence of auto accidents, school dropouts, and violence, etc. Furthermore, there is no debate among researchers that marijuana is both psychologically and physically addictive, especially for adolescents and young adults. Does this sound safe and benign?

- The most common drug for which users seek treatment help is marijuana.[9]
- There were 375,000 emergency hospital visits involving marijuana.[7]
- Marijuana is the leading cause of substance dependence other than alcohol.[2]

Q: *With the de facto legalization, or total legalization of marijuana, how much would use increase?*

That is a difficult question to answer, as one cannot positively predict the exact percentage of increase. The most commonly quoted figure based on other legalization experiments is that it would likely double. Another important question to ask is how much of an increased use is acceptable so that a small minority of our population can get stoned with impunity. The answer should be *none*. It only takes one incident to cause death of a son, daughter, husband, or wife in a head-on collision because somebody drove under the influence of marijuana. Many responsible and caring people would forgo alcohol if the eleven thousand moms, dads, children, aunts, uncles, grandparents who are killed every year by a drunk driver could be spared. Accidents from marijuana-impaired driving are relatively common.

The impairing effect of cannabis use on driving can continue much longer than that of alcohol. Cannabis users can experience flashbacks several weeks after taking cannabis. Roughly a quarter of cannabis users experience some kind of flashback.

Q: *Given the poor state of our economy, wouldn't taxing marijuana dispensaries boost our government's income?*

Taxing marijuana would create additional revenue. However, experience shows the additional revenue would not even come close to offsetting additional costs associated with increased use. The two legal substances which are highly taxed prove the point. Taxes on alcohol account for $14.5 billion in revenue, but alcohol abuse costs $185 billion.[7] In the case of tobacco, taxes account for $25 billion, but the cost to society is $200 billion.[7] That means taxes pay for 8 percent and 12 percent respectively for all the adverse effects of alcohol and tobacco use. It doesn't require a degree in economics to understand a poor investment. One can reasonably expect the same type of figures with marijuana taxation.

Q: *Cannot the marijuana distribution centers or dispensaries in Colorado be regulated to eliminate the abuse?*

Under the current law, there is no way to regulate the dispensaries or marijuana-distribution industry to eliminate abuse and the impact of de facto legalization. These marijuana centers can grow six marijuana plants or possess two ounces per patient. There is no way of verifying how often a patient purchases marijuana, which patient(s) they are growing for, how much goes out the backdoor, how much they are giving to other dispensaries, etc., unless they have an inspector on site at each dispensary. There are not enough investigators or inspectors to thoroughly regulate the industry that is motivated by profit. There is also no way to control the marijuana once it is purchased. According to a treatment providers and school resource officers, many teens admit getting their marijuana from cardholders.

Q: *Since marijuana distribution centers in Colorado are against federal law, what are the ramifications to jurisdictions that not only allow but attempt in some manner to regulate them?*

Under federal law, marijuana distribution centers are criminal enterprises engaged in the distribution of a schedule I controlled substance which is contraband. Federal law preempts state law. Jurisdictions that allow and attempt to regulate these centers are putting themselves and their employees in a position of aiding and abetting a criminal enterprise. The money these centers make from selling marijuana is illegally gained assets and thus subject to seizure. For a jurisdiction to take a portion of those funds for fees or taxes is effectively using illegally gained funds and laundering them. The state, cities, and/or counties are aiding and abetting criminal enterprises. This is contrary to the principles upon which this country, governed by laws, was built.

Q: *What groups would generally oppose and what groups generally favor dispensaries?*

The witnesses at the Colorado state capitol testifying against the dispensary model as a part of HR 1284 were drug-abuse experts from treatment, prevention/education, and law enforcement. The witnesses in favor of dispensaries and loose regulations were the dispensary owners, some "patients," and those who favored marijuana legalization.

Q: *What is the upside of local jurisdictions banning dispensaries?*

Below are the positive aspects of banning dispensaries in the local jurisdiction.

- The city and/or county would be honoring the intent of the majority of voters who approved Amendment 20 as a patient/caregiver model and not marijuana distribution centers.
- The city and/or county would be honoring and respecting federal law as opposed to sanctioning federal law violators. Additionally, the city and/or county would be respecting the laws of the majority of the states in this nation.

- The city and/or county would not be sending out a hypocritical message as it relates to drug abuse education in its schools.
- The city and/or county would be eliminating the cost of policing and responding to crime and incidents at the marijuana distribution centers.
- The city and/or county would be sending a clear message to its citizens and youth that drug abuse is not okay in its jurisdiction.
- The citizens and youth would not have to be concerned about seeing marijuana glorified by storefronts and/or advertisements in their community.
- The city or county officials would be heeding the advice of their drug abuse experts not only in law enforcement but also treatment and prevention that dispensaries are de facto legalization which will lead to increased drug abuse in their community.
- The city or county officials, in these tight economic times, would not have to deal with the additional cost of increased marijuana use through calls for police services, accidents, treatment, hospital emergency admissions, adverse incidents in schools, increased dropouts, etc.
- The city or county officials would truly be doing their part to make their communities drug free.

Q: *What is the downside to banning dispensaries?*

- The few legitimate patients in the community might have to travel a little further to get their medical marijuana as would primary caregivers for the homebound, legitimate medical marijuana patients.
- The city or county ban may initially upset dispensary owners and marijuana users who might stage protests.
- The marijuana legalizers and dispensary owners most likely will sue over the constitutionality of HR 1284 as well as the banning of dispensaries in local jurisdictions.

The district attorney for the Eighth Judicial District, Larry Abrahamson, identified the unintended consequences in a public letter on June 10, 2010, that states,

In 2000, Colorado voters approved an initiative that permitted the use of marijuana as a medical aid in easing the pain and discomfort experienced from specific chronic or debilitating diseases. After all, why shouldn't a doctor be able to authorize marijuana? It seemed to make sense to many—as long as it was restricted to six or less plants and under two ounces of processed marijuana in the user's possession. Since initiatives do not afford the benefit of debate and testimony that the legislative process provides, many did not see the unintended consequences looming on the horizon. Although law enforcement and district attorneys, including now-Attorney General John Suthers, were vocal about the possible adverse impacts, the amendment still passed. In retrospect, they may have been right in nearly every aspect of their prediction.

The unintended consequences:

1. A loosely defined "primary caregiver" was interpreted as a person supplying marijuana to another.
2. Doctors were charging up to $500 per authorization without physicals or verification of the severe pain.
3. The six-plant-two-ounce maximum was being ignored by new establishments called dispensaries.
4. Dispensaries were protected by confidentiality rules in the Department of Health from revealing the names of their patients, thus thwarting law enforcement efforts to detect violations and abuses.
5. No quality control or testing standards for marijuana strength, dosage, or frequency of use.
6. "The number of medical marijuana applications the state received on January 12, 2010, was a whopping 1,650—an all-time record for one day," says state registrar Ron Hyman, who oversees the applications. Colorado had about 5000 at the end of 2009.
7. Some of the marijuana was being supplied by cartels out of Mexico in order to keep up with demand.
8. Local police departments reported an increase in violent home invasion crimes, with money or drugs being sought.
9. The "severe pain" condition was not defined, thus 91% claim severe pain as their reason for needing marijuana.

10. Municipalities were being flooded with requests for sales tax license for their new dispensary business. Approximately 150 approved in Larimer County.
11. Dispensary owners will undoubtedly challenge the state's authority to regulate any part of their business beyond what they believe the Constitutional Amendment allows.

Under the new law, there is some tightening of the rules, but the dispensary concept—now called "centers," is still alive. Cities will be allowed to Opt Out of the provision that allows centers to operate within their boundaries. Council members in any community should consider the following:

a. Is there an impact on our children regularly seeing an illegal drug, marijuana, being advertised as a helpful medicine?
b. Are there other valid intrinsic reasons that should be considered?
c. Are there potential abuses by centers as was seen before the latest statute was passed?
d. Is this a business the citizens want to encourage when it is still a violation of federal law?
e. Do allowing marijuana centers leave visitors with a positive impression of our city?
f. Consider the increase in home invasions, is there a public safety factor that should concern our citizens.
g. Were "centers" anticipated under the amendment or were voters thinking that the amendment would simply protect a person who, while under a doctor's care, wanted to grow and use marijuana for medicinal purposes?

As always, policy discussions have to be made by weighing the benefits against the cost to the citizens. Let your city council representatives know how you want them to handle the commercial distribution of Marijuana in our community.

The continued abuse of any system that the government puts in place is inevitable. Unfortunately, with MMDs, the propensity of abuse escalates even more because of the easy access and lack of screening for patients. On December 9, 2011, the *Denver Post* reported, "Some

4,200 medical marijuana applications in Colorado are on hold at the state health department while investigators look at possible fraud.

"The Colorado Department of Public Health and Environment announced Friday that marijuana registry applications from certain physicians are on hold after law-enforcement officials witnessed potential patients being seen by someone other than a physician. Colorado law requires a bona fide doctor-patient relationship before a physician can recommend marijuana pot for certain ailments."

On March 23, 2012, the Larimer County Sheriff's Office in Fort Collins, Colorado, sent out a press release regarding two medical doctors that were arrested for issuing fraudulent medical marijuana recommendations. The press release is as follows:

FOR IMMEDIATE RELEASE

Contact: Larimer County Sheriff's Office
John Schulz, Public Information Officer
Public Information Office: 970-980-2501

Subject: Doctors Arrested for False Medical Marijuana
Recommendations
Date: 4/27/2012

On March 22, 2012, Dr. Dallas Williams of Milliken, a seventy-three-year-old male who practices medicine at the InHarmony Wellness Center in Windsor, Colorado, and Dr. Joseph Montante of Longmont, a sixty-three-year-old male who practices medicine at the Dr. Green Blossom Wellness Center in Loveland, Colorado, were arrested by the Larimer County Sheriff's Office for investigation of attempting to influence a public servant, a class-four felony.

These arrests were based on an undercover investigation involving members of the Larimer County Sheriff's Office Criminal Impact Unit, investigators from the North Metro Drug Task Force, and the Colorado Attorney General's Office.

This investigation was initiated after investigators received information that both doctors were issuing medical marijuana recommendations to clients with knowledge that the clients did not suffer from a debilitating medical condition. Colorado law limits the use of medical marijuana to those who suffer from legally defined "debilitating medical conditions." Based on this information, undercover investigators initiated contact with both doctors and were able to obtain recommendations for medical marijuana after clearly stating they had no debilitating medical conditions which would authorize them to obtain medical marijuana.

Arrest warrants were issued for both doctors based on this investigation. Dr. Dallas Williams and Dr. Joseph Montante were arrested, booked at the Larimer County Jail, and later released after posting $3,500 personal recognizance bonds.

This case has been turned over to the Larimer County District Attorney's Office for prosecution.

The charge(s) are merely an accusation, and the defendant is presumed innocent until and unless proven guilty.

No additional information will be released.

###END###

Another press release from the Larimer County Sheriff's Office on April 12, 2012, clearly illustrates how the MMD industry has become a new *black market* for selling marijuana. The following press release was sent to me:

FOR IMMEDIATE RELEASE

Contact: Larimer County Sheriff's Office
          John Schulz, Public Information Officer
          Public Information Office—970-980-2501

Subject: Marijuana Grow House Shut Down
Date: 4/12/2012

Larimer County Sheriff's Office investigators arrested Ryan Conrad-Davis, DOB: 051085, of Fort Collins last night (041112) on charges of cultivating, possessing and distributing marijuana, all felonies. Conrad-Davis was also charged as a special offender as his sole source of income was from the drug operation. The arrest took place at 705 South Taft Hill Road.

Larimer County investigators were informed about the grow operation by Georgia law enforcement officials who believe that Conrad-Davis moved to Colorado specifically to operate a grow facility and mail the marijuana back to Georgia for sale.

Investigators seized 25 live plants, several ounces of processed marijuana, a small quantity of psilocybin mushrooms as well as distribution paraphernalia like a digital scale, baggies, etc.

Conrad-Davis was arrested without incident and booked into the Larimer County Jail where he is being held pending a court hearing to determine his bond.

The investigation is ongoing to determine if other arrests are warranted.

The charge(s) are merely an accusation and the defendant is presumed innocent until and unless proven guilty.

###END###

While the Sheriff's Office was arresting illegal grow operations, people who own some of the MMDs were at Fort Collins City Hall, filing for another petition for a special election to reverse the initial election in November 2011. Kirk Scramstad filed with the City Clerk's Office a *Notice of Intent to Circulate an Initiative Petition*. Mr. Scramstad (previously associated with the medical marijuana dispensary "A Kind Place") was accompanied by Mark Belkin, Organizing Director of the Unified Food and Commercial Workers Union, Local 7.

The Notice of Intent requests a special election to be held in conjunction with the November General Election of 2012. This is a never ending story.

Chapter 4 Endnotes

1. Alcoholism, SAMHSA Health Information Network
2. Dr. Robert DuPont, former director of NIDA Community, April 20, 2010, commentary
3. American Lung Association, February 2010 Report
4. University of Michigan Study, 2010 for NIDA
5. 2010 National Drug Threat Assessment
6. National Highway Traffic Safety Administration, 2008
7. ONDCP Director Gil Kerlikowske Statement, March 4, 2010
8. National Drug Control Strategy, February 2007
9. Treatment Episode Data Set Highlights, 2009, SAMHSA
10. (Prolong effects after smoking marijuana-driving and flashbacks) Cannabis—Hash and Marijuana—A factsheet from the Swedish Council for Information on Alcohol and other drugs, see at 19 March 2002. See also Hollister, L E, 'Health Aspects of Cannabis', Pharmacological Reviews, 38(1), 1986, page 7; Ashton, C H, 'Ad http://www.can.se/showStandard.asp?id=27verse effects of cannabis and cannabinoids', Op cit, pages 637-649
11. Flashbacks with marijuana use, See www.drugscope.org.uk/druginformation/drugsearch/ds_results.asp?file=\wip\11\1\1\flashbacks.htm as at 19 March 2002
12. *Thousands of Colo. marijuana applications on hold—Denver Post http://www.denverpost.com/news/marijuana/ci_19509992?IADID=Search-www.denverpost.com-www.denverpost.com#ixzz1pyzKIKVZ*
13. Larimer County Sheriff's Office press release received from *Sheriff-Press-Release [sheriff-press-release@co.larimer.co.us]*, March 23, 2012

CHAPTER 5

The Campaign—Citywide

Photo by Ray Martinez; billboard site was at Prospect and College Ave.,
Fort Collins, CO (bright orange with white letters)

When the committee Concerned Fort Collins Citizens formed together
and registered as an official campaign organization with the City of Fort
Collins, we identified some *key* points to address and get the message
out to the voters. Our slogan was "Let's be honest . . ." The intentions
and information we addressed were based on truth and facts in order to
win the ballot Initiative 300.

We had close to a dozen core members who met weekly to keep the
campaign operating smoothly. Like many other campaigns, we needed
to know what the opposition was doing and yet do our own preparations,

i.e. billboards, newspaper ads, arranging for door-to-door knocking, flyers, brochures, fundraising, and speaking to various organizations and groups of people. The supporters came from all walks of life; even some were people who used marijuana for medicinal purposes. Those who were using medical marijuana (MM) and supporting us were upset about the deceit being used by the opposition.

Our first step in the process was to secure a legal petition from the city to circulate and collect over 4,214 signatures; the number of required signatures is based on a percentage of the previous number of votes cast in the last election. On the average, about 25 percent of the collected signatures are usually rendered invalid for various reasons. Some people think they live in the city limits but don't. Others did not realize they were not registered to vote, and some people just want to sign the petition.

The committee consisted of some very sincere, honest community builders and leaders of Fort Collins, which I was very proud to be a part of the group. We decided from the onset that the collection of signatures guidelines was essential to follow, not only to acquire good signatures, but to save ourselves a lot of time and effort. The window of opportunity was short, so time was of the essence to us.

Unsurprisingly, all of the needed signatures were collected. In fact, we secured 7,579 signatures as a good safety margin. When all was done, we learned that approximately 12 percent of the signatures were rejected; that's unheard of and well done!

Some of the locations that we were collecting signatures, people were lining up to sign up!

The only struggle I and others saw with the ballot language was that the voter had to vote yes on ballot 300 to vote against the medical marijuana dispensaries (MMDs), which may have caused some confusion for many voters. The natural inclination is to vote no on something you do not want. Several people called me up, questioning which way was the correct way to vote against the MMDs. So I am certain this had a bearing on the accuracy of the voter turnout.

The election was a real "nail-biter" because of our concern of the ballot language. However, at the end of the day, the voters decided to close the MMDs, but we only won by a 2 percent margin. If I was to compare to the amount of signatures were received for the petition drive, the telephone calls I received before and after the election, I am convinced that the winning margin would have been much larger if the ballot language was more clear or switched to vote "no" versus "yes."

Some of the campaign messages are as follows:

Let's be honest . . .

Pot shops, marijuana grows, and marijuana candy are illegal enterprises; the intent of the voters in adopting Amendment 20 has not been honored

In July 2011, the U.S. attorney general made it very clear that the operation of any aspect of a medical marijuana enterprise is a federal crime and reclarified that marijuana is an illegal drug. The term "medical marijuana" is inherently deceptive, since marijuana is *not* a drug proven to be a safe, effective medication; is not approved by the Food and Drug Administration (FDA) for safe consumption; cannot be prescribed by physicians; and cannot be controlled or dispensed by a pharmacist. The medical marijuana industry is shrouded in a myriad of misunderstandings, deceptions, and illegalities.

- Federal law preempts state law and state constitutional amendments.
- MMDs are classified as criminal enterprises by the federal government.
- Persons who cultivate, sell, distribute, or facilitate commercial marijuana storefronts are violating the Controlled Substances Act.
- Public employees are currently abetting criminal enterprises.
- Taxing marijuana sales is a criminal activity identified as money laundering.
- Intent of voters in adopting Amendment 20 has not been honored: marijuana lobbyists influenced misguided legislation, House Bill 1284

Voters did not intend for Amendment 20 to become a disguise for the de facto legalization of marijuana. "In 2000, there was no public discussion about retail pot outlets, or the *wink-and-nod* atmosphere that now exists in which thousands of people have claimed chronic, debilitating pain in order to get medical marijuana registry cards (*Denver Post*, August 28, 2011)."

- MMDs are a distortion of the voter-approved constitutional amendment, which allows seriously ill people to possess marijuana for medicinal purposes.
- Voters did not vote to allow the retail sale of marijuana through a mass distribution system that is being severely abused by those who are not truly suffering from a tragic illness.
- Closing marijuana stores will not restrict patients from growing their own marijuana or having a caregiver grow marijuana for them (per Amendment 20).
- There are sixteen thousand caregivers (not including dispensaries) registered with State Board of Health who can grow marijuana for patients with an MMJ card.
- Patients can call the Department of Public Health for names and contact information for registered caregivers.
- There were only five thousand patients on the State Registry throughout the state from 2000-2009, until marijuana lobbyists swayed the health board to lift the five-patient limit per caregiver in 2009. This removal of the five-patient limit allowed the explosion of dispensaries and led to the medical marijuana (MMJ) lobbyists' victory with the misguided legislation of House Bill 1284.
- There are 130,000 medical marijuana (MMJ) card holders in Colorado with 1,100 new applicants per day just prior to this publication.
- The average age of MMJ patients is only forty years old and 69 percent of the patients are male.
- How ironic that 94 percent of patients on the MMJ registry report "severe pain" as their illness and only 6 percent use marijuana for cancer, glaucoma, AIDS, and other debilitating illnesses.

Fifteen physicians, several of whom were sanctioned and could no longer prescribe medications, provided 76 percent of MMJ recommendations for patients throughout the entire State of Colorado (Director Thomas J. Gorman, Rocky Mountain High Intensity Drug Trafficking Area, referencing the *Denver Post*, 2010). See chapter 7 regarding two medical doctors arrested for issuing medical marijuana recommendations to clients with knowledge that the clients did not suffer from a debilitating medical condition.

Citizens of Fort Collins are urged to vote to ban these illegal enterprises. The caregiver model, outlined in Amendment 20, worked effectively in 2000 to 2009, granting patients legal protection to use marijuana for medicinal purposes. As stated in Amendment 20, patients on the MMJ registry may either grow their own marijuana or receive it from a "primary Caregiver who is significantly involved with the patient's care (per Colorado Court of Appeals ruling)."

Door hanger flyer used during the campaign
to inform the public about the truth

Since ballot 300 was won in Fort Collins, I get the impression that the city council and staff members are seeking away to circumvent the voters' direction by expanding the amount of caregivers that can conduct growing operations. The City of Fort Collins is already putting out a Monkey Survey, asking if citizens want to expand the trade under a different name or system. This is a real slap in the face to the voters who already ordered the selling operations to close.

You may recall that state legislators clarified the role of a caregiver in their most recent legislation: "The act of supplying medical marijuana or marijuana paraphernalia, by itself, is insufficient to constitute 'significant responsibility for managing the well-being of a patient.'"

Knowing this, all prior medical marijuana distributers should be disqualified as potential caregivers unless they meet the criteria of a caregiver. Perhaps that will take away the catalyst for city council's actions to facilitate the growth of more marijuana within the City of Fort Collins. Let's save a little taxpayer money and stop another one of the city's "studies and outreach to citizens" until they get the answer they want.

The following is an in-house memorandum from the city's Neighborhood Services Department staff, Ginny Sawyer, neighborhood administrator of Medical Marijuana Staff Team, to the city manager, Darin Atteberry, that clearly signals the idea of skirting around the voters' direction:

DATE: March 26, 2012

TO: Darin Atteberry, City Manager

FROM: Ginny Sawyer, Neighborhood Administrator
        Medical Marijuana Staff Team

RE: Current Outreach Plan

Overview

The medical marijuana staff team was in front of City Council in February 2012 with items related to changing code to reflect the recent ballot initiative and clarifying regulations regarding growing in multi-family housing. At the February 21, 2012 meeting the topic of allowing/or not allowing additional growing locations was discussed.

At that meeting and following, staff felt they had clear direction to move forward with an extensive and timely outreach plan. Please see below for:

1. February 21, 2012 meeting minutes
2. Existing Survey and outreach timeline

If there is something additional Leadership would like to see as part of this outreach effort, please let us know.

Meeting Minutes

The following is reflected in the February 21, 2012 minutes:

The second issue that staff has been directed to pursue has to do with the areas of the City in which medical marijuana may be cultivated by primary caregivers and patients. In response to the voter-approved ban on medical marijuana businesses that went into effect February 14, 2012, Ordinance No. 010, 2012, amends the City's Land Use Code to delete all references to such businesses. The effect of this amendment to the LUC is that residential dwelling units will now be the only locations in the City where medical marijuana may be cultivated. At the hearing on First Reading, several primary caregivers and one of their representatives asked that Council reconsider this situation and make available additional areas in the City where they and their patients may lawfully cultivate medical marijuana.

Current Outreach Plan

Based on Council direction to do outreach and the desire to keep it timely staff has developed the following timeline:

- Late March/early April -general survey
- Last week in April- focus group
- May 17, Planning and Zoning Board (materials due May 2)
- June 5, City Council (materials due May 23)

Staff developed a four question survey which can be viewed here:

https://www.surveymonkey.com/s/mmj1p

A copy of the survey is also attached.

To date, the survey has been distributed to the following:

- North and South Fort Collins Business Associations

- Commercial Real Estate agents (through Sperry Van Ness)

- CityWorks Alumni

- Medical marijuana advocates (through previous business owners and citizens who emailed City Leaders prior to the February 21 meeting)

- The Larimer County Medical Society (700 member organization)

- The Northern Colorado Rental Housing Association

The survey will also be available on fcgov.com starting in April.

Based on survey feedback, focus group outcome, and staff research staff will be working on crafting recommendation to take to both the Planning and Zoning Board and City Council.

memo to the City Manager Darin Atteberry—planning outreach to secure survey. Memo excludes Concerned Fort Collins Citizens committee. Why?

Jim and Nancy Patella of Fort Collins, Colorado, community advocates, provided some good points of discussion that the citizens of Fort Collins should inquire about with the city staff and city council members.

1) The marijuana suppliers are disingenuous in their medical claims in their store names and in their claims of how many true patients they are treating. Why do we still accept the claims of

these people who are trying to take advantage of a compassioned vote in 2000 to fatten their wallets?

2) City council asked in council meetings last year how we were going to treat the 8,512 patients on the registry who need medicine. There are now 4,828 patients on the registry. The quantity of patients has almost been cut in half, perhaps because of less availability in Larimer County. Do we still believe all of those people are patients, even if we cast aside the "debilitating condition" requirement?

3) Why can't we consider last November's Question 300 vote to be the "outreach" program? Sending a survey to a subset of the voting public that contradicts the ordinance the voters passed in November is a breach of our system of democracy.

4) Are we to believe the marijuana suppliers or our county sheriff when we hear from the suppliers that neighborhoods will be less safe if we don't grow more marijuana? Growing marijuana in commercial areas will not reduce neighborhood grows. It will just increase the supply of marijuana in the city. Commercial areas are not that far away from neighborhoods or schools or churches.

5) Research proves "the terrible carnage out there on the roads caused by marijuana." More marijuana makes our neighborhoods and citizens more unsafe.

6) Area business owners have concerns about marijuana's effects upon employee and customer safety.

7) Prior marijuana business owners cannot become caregivers unless they follow state law (federal law, of course, is being ignored in all of this and apparently doesn't count). State law strictly states that a caregiver must regularly assist a patient with activities of daily living. The act of supplying medical marijuana or marijuana paraphernalia, by itself, is insufficient to constitute "significant responsibility for managing the well-being of a patient."

8) Who is pressuring the city to facilitate the growth of more marijuana?

9) City staff felt they had clear direction to move forward with an extensive and timely outreach plan as a result of the February 2012 council meeting. Extensive sounds like expensive. Why not save taxpayer money or spend it on educational programs

to counteract the damage done by the false advertising and
marketing of marijuana stores? This would reduce abuse and
leave more marijuana for the patients that truly need it, so more
marijuana would not need to be grown.

References provided by Jim and Nancy Patella:

http://www.cdphe.state.co.us/hs/medicalmarijuana/statistics.html
Larimer County registry:
June, 2011: 8,512 patients on the registry
December, 2011: 4,828 patients on the registry

Colorado Department of Education:
http://www.cde.state.co.us/DropoutPrevention/Resources.htm

Coloradoan, "States Grapple with Limits for Stone Driving," 3/19/12.
Coloradoan, "Tale of Two Cities," 2/14/12.

Question 300 Ballot Language

Section 1. Pursuant to Article 43.3 of Title 12 of the Colorado Revised
    Statutes, the City of Fort Collins hereby prohibits the operation of
    Medical Marijuana Centers, Optional Premises Cultivation Operations
    and Medical Marijuana Infused Products Manufacturing, effective ten
    (10) days following publication of the within Ordinance as provided in
    Section 4.9 (B) of the Home Rule Charter of the City of Fort Collins. With
    respect to any such Centers, Operations, facilities or businesses of any
    kind in operation upon such effective date, each and every such Center,
    Operation, facility and business shall cease operations within ninety (90)
    days of said date.
Section 2. Should the City Council refer this Initiated Ordinance to the
    registered electors of the City at a regular or special municipal election,
    this Initiated Ordinance shall take effect immediately upon certification by
    the designated election official that a majority of registered electors voted
    in favor of this Initiated Ordinance at such regular or special election.
    In such event, each and every Medical Marijuana Centers, Optional
    Premises Cultivation Operations and Medical Marijuana Infused Products
    Manufacturing in operation on such effective date shall cease operations
    within ninety (90) days of the effective date specified in this Section 2.

http://www.cdphe.state.co.us/regulations/vitalstatistics/100602medicalus
emarijuana.pdf
DEPARTMENT OF PUBLIC HEALTH AND ENVIRONMENT
Health and Environmental Information and Statistics Division 5 CCR
1006-2
MEDICAL USE OF MARIJUANA
(PROMULGATED BY THE STATE BOARD OF HEALTH)
Last amended 11/16/11, effective 12/30/11

Excerpt regarding caregivers

"Primary care-giver" means a person other than the patient and the
patient's physician, who is eighteen years of age or older and has
significant responsibility for managing the well-being of a patient who
has a debilitating medical condition. A person shall be listed as a primary
care-giver for no more than five patients in the medical marijuana program
registry at any given time unless a waiver has been granted for exceptional
circumstances, as per Regulation Ten below. iii) "Significant responsibility
for managing the well-being of a patient" means, in addition to the ability
to provide medical marijuana, regularly assisting a patient with activities
of daily living, including but not limited to transportation or housekeeping
or meal preparation or shopping or making any necessary arrangement for
access to medical care or other services unrelated to medical marijuana.
The act of supplying medical marijuana or marijuana paraphernalia, by
itself, is insufficient to constitute "significant responsibility for managing
the well-being of a patient."

Medical Marijuana Businesses
are Illegal Enterprises under Federal Law

According to federal law, which preempts state law, dispensaries are
criminal enterprises.

Persons who are in the business of cultivating, selling, or distributing
marijuana, and those who knowingly facilitate (conspire, aid, abet) such
activities are in violation of the Controlled Substances Act, regardless
of state law. State laws or local ordinances are not a defense to civil or
criminal enforcement of federal law with respect to such conduct.

Public employees who collect taxes or inspect are wrong for conspiring, aiding, and abetting a criminal enterprise, and are engaged in felonies.

Taxing marijuana sales is essentially money laundering. Should enforcement action take place, the federal government can seize dispensary contents, profits, and taxes (including retroactively). Tax revenues from marijuana sales collected by the City of Fort Collins may be in jeopardy of being forfeited; it may be illegal money collected from the illicit sale of an illegal drug.

I am amazed that Colorado lawmakers are allowing several new initiatives to legalize marijuana, knowing that federal law prohibits it. Federal law trumps state law, which the U.S. Supreme Court has ruled on a number of times. The current proposed initiatives at the time of this publication are:

Proposed Initiative No. 70 would make it a constitutional right to possess up to four ounces of marijuana for people 21 and older. The initiative would also allow for marijuana to be sold in stores that are regulated like tobacco businesses.

Proposed Initiative No. 65 would give doctors discretion to recommend marijuana for any medical condition.

Regulate Marijuana Like Alcohol Act of 2012 would legalize possession of up to an ounce of marijuana for people twenty-one and older and allow adults to grow up to six marijuana plants in their homes. The measure also allows for pot shops; this measure qualified for the ballot with enough signatures required by law.

The following two proposed initiatives legalize possession of any amount:

> *Relief for the Possession of Cannabis Act* would prohibit judges from imposing penalties on anyone for marijuana possession."

Legalize 2012 would create in Colorado's constitution a fundamental right to marijuana for people eighteen and older and would also allow for retail marijuana sales."

One person who really helped kick off the campaign and bring out the importance of addressing this issue of medical marijuana is Dr. Nancy Smith. Her passion and compassion for our youth is extraordinary. All of the people involved with the committee only had one objective in mind—protect our youth, which is our future, and the patients who honestly need medication. We also wanted the truth to be known about marijuana and that our city council operates within the parameters of the law, including federal laws.

I couldn't express Dr. Smith's feelings any better without sharing her e-mail message to me.

"After having had a psychotherapy practice in Dallas for twenty five years, I relocated to Colorado and founded the Center for Family Care in Ft. Collins in 2006. My commitment to Ft. Collins youth begins with my grandchildren and extends to all of the children and teenagers in my counseling practice and the youth throughout the city. In late 2009 and early 2010, I detected a dramatic shift in the attitude among my teenage clients regarding marijuana and discovered a renewed loyalty to their "Don't Ask . . . Don't Tell" rule (regarding pot). I was alarmed and puzzled about their new interest and intrigue with marijuana. Then, I realized what the "buzz" was all about . . . the sudden explosion of the medical marijuana industry in our city. The visible presence of the dispensaries was conveying the widespread message to your youth that marijuana is a "medicine . . . a harmless herb" causing youth to no longer fear using pot and making it easy for them to get access to the drug due to the over-abundant supply made available by the large number of dispensaries and grow operations throughout the city.

"My heart sank. I flashed back to the 80s when teenage drug abuse was rampant...when there were no prevention programs, no intervention programs and no treatment programs for our youth. As a young therapist back then, I had treated lots of young people whose lives were drastically compromised and some whose lives were lost before the nation began to take action to develop drug prevention, intervention and treatment programs for the nation's youth. I knew that the medical marijuana industry had the power to seduce our youth into believing that "pot" was not a dangerous, addictive drug, but merely an herb with magical medicinal powers that could give them incredible 'highs' and relief from the stress of teenage life.

"Once I realized that the marijuana industry had masterfully swept in and created a new image of marijuana as a safe sustainer of life, I made a commitment to do whatever I could, regardless of the emotional, physical and personal cost, to protect our youth and the community at large from an industry that was destined to threaten the immediate and future health of our children and youth and the well-being of our city. Therefore, I helped organize and mobilize a group of concerned citizens (the Concerned Fort Collins Citizens) who conducted a Petition Initiative and educational campaign which resulted in the voters of Ft. Collins voting to ban the medical marijuana industry from operation in Ft. Collins."

"I am grateful to be a part of this conjoint effort, which proved to be one of the most exhausting, exhilarating and fulfilling experiences of my life."

Nancy Smith, PhD, LPC

Nancy R. Smith, PhD, received her doctorate in Counseling at the University of North Texas, Denton, Texas. She is a licensed professional counselor (LPC) in Colorado, and is the founding director of the Center for Family Care, Ft. Collins, Colorado, where she conducts a private practice, specializing in therapy with children, adolescents, and families. Dr. Smith had a private practice in Dallas, Texas, for nearly thirty years, before relocating to Ft. Collins, Colorado. Dr. Smith has developed and published a psychodynamic group model for children and adolescents and has coauthored an instructional video series, "Enter the World of Play Therapy, I and II," *used in the training of graduate students in various universities throughout the country. In the mid-80s, she organized a community-wide task force which sponsored a city-wide symposium, Dallas Challenge, which led to the formation of Dallas Challenge (a 501 c 3 non-profit) that funded alcohol—and drug-intervention counselors in thirty schools in the Dallas Independent School District. Dallas Challenge continues today to provide drug prevention and drug intervention services to youth and their families within the Dallas metroplex.*

On April 26, 2011, the United States Attorney, District of Colorado, John F. Walsh, wrote a letter to Colorado Attorney General John Suthers, regarding the U.S. Attorney Generals stance on Colorado marijuana distribution.

U.S. DEPARTMENT OF JUSTICE

John F. Walsh

United States Attorney
District of Colorado

1225 Seventeenth Street, Suite 700   *303-454-0100*
Seventeenth Street Plaza   (FAX)   *303-454-0400*
Denver, Colorado 80202

April 26, 2011

John Suthers
Attorney General
State of Colorado
1525 Sherman St., 7th Floor
Denver, CO 80203

Dear Attorney General Suthers:

I am writing in response to your request for clarification of the position of the U.S. Department of Justice (the "Department") with respect to activities that would be licensed or otherwise permitted under the terms of pending House Bill 1043 in the Colorado General Assembly. I have consulted with the Attorney General of the United States and the Deputy Attorney General of the United States about this bill, and write to ensure that there is no confusion as to the Department's views on such activities.

As the Department has noted on many prior occasions, the Congress of the United States has determined that marijuana is a controlled substance, and has placed marijuana on Schedule I of the Controlled Substances Act (CSA). Federal law under Title 21 of the United States Code, Section 841, prohibits the manufacture, distribution or possession with intent to distribute any controlled substance, including marijuana, except as provided under the strict control provisions of the CSA. Title 21, Section 856 makes it a federal crime to lease, rent or maintain a place for the purpose of manufacturing, distributing or using a controlled substance. Title 21, Section 846 makes it a federal crime to conspire to commit that crime, or any other crime under the CSA. Title 18, Section 2 makes it a federal crime to aid and abet the commission of a federal crime. Moreover, federal anti-money laundering statutes, including Title 18, Section 1956, make illegal certain financial transactions designed to promote illegal activities, including drug trafficking, or to conceal or disguise the source of the proceeds of that illegal activity. Title 18, Section 1957, makes it illegal to engage in a financial transaction involving more than $10,000 in criminal proceeds.

In October 2009, the Department issued guidance (the "Ogden Memo") to U.S. Attorneys around the country in states with laws authorizing the use of marijuana for medical purposes

John Suthers
April 26, 2011
Page 2

under state law. At the time the Ogden Memo issued, Colorado law, and specifically, Amendment 20 to the Colorado Constitution, authorized the possession of only very limited amounts of marijuana for medical purposes by individuals with serious illnesses and those who care for them.[1] As reiterated in the Ogden memo, the prosecution of individuals and organizations involved in the trade of any illegal drugs and the disruption of drug trafficking organizations is a core priority of the Department. This core priority includes prosecution of business enterprises that unlawfully market and sell marijuana. Accordingly, while the Department does not focus its limited resources on seriously ill individuals who use marijuana as part of a medically recommended treatment regimen in compliance with state law as stated in the Ogden Memo, we maintain the authority to enforce the CSA vigorously against individuals and organizations that participate in unlawful manufacturing and distribution activity involving marijuana, even if such activities are permitted under state law. The Department's investigative and prosecutorial resources will continue to be directed toward these objectives.

It is well settled that a State cannot authorize violations of federal law. The United States District Court for the District of Colorado recently reaffirmed this fundamental principle of our federal constitutional system in *United States v. Bartkowicz*, No. 10-cr-00118-PAB (D. Colo. 2010), when it held that Colorado state law on medical marijuana does not and cannot alter federal law's prohibition on the manufacture, distribution or possession of marijuana, or provide a defense to prosecution under federal law for such activities.

The provisions of Colorado House Bill 1043, if enacted, would permit under state law conduct that is contrary to federal law, and would threaten the ability of the United States government to regulate possession, manufacturing and trafficking in controlled substances, including marijuana. First, provisions of a proposed medical marijuana investment fund amendment to H.B. 1043, which ultimately did not pass in the Colorado House but which apparently may be reintroduced as an amendment in the Colorado Senate, appear to contemplate that the State of Colorado would license a marijuana investment fund or funds under which both Colorado and out-of-state investors would invest in commercial marijuana operations. The Department would consider civil and criminal legal remedies regarding those who invest in the production of marijuana, which is in violation of federal law, even if the investment is made in a state-licensed fund of the kind proposed.

Second, the terms of H.B. 1043 would authorize Colorado state licensing of "medical marijuana infused product" facilities with up to 500 marijuana plants, with the possibility of licensing even larger facilities, with no stated number limit, with a state-granted waiver based upon consideration of broad factors such as "business need." Similarly, the Department would consider civil actions and criminal prosecution regarding those who set up marijuana growing facilities and dispensaries, as well as property owners, as they will be acting in violation of federal law.

---

[1] As passed by Colorado voters in 2000, Amendment 20 made lawful under Colorado law the possession by a patient or caregiver of patient of "[n]o more than two ounces of a useable form of marijuana or no more than six marijuana plants with three or fewer being mature, flowering plants producing a usable form of marijuana." Colo. Const. art. XVIII, § 14(4)(a). Within these limits, the Amendment authorized a medical marijuana "affirmative defense" to state criminal prosecution for possession of marijuana. Colo. Const. art. XVIII, § 14(2)(a), (b).

John Suthers
April 26, 2011
Page 3

As the Attorney General has repeatedly stated, the Department of Justice remains firmly committed to enforcing the federal law and the Controlled Substances Act in all states. Thus, if the provisions of H.B. 1043 are enacted and become law, the Department will continue to carefully consider all appropriate civil and criminal legal remedies to prevent manufacture and distribution of marijuana and other associated violations of federal law, including injunctive actions; civil penalties; criminal prosecution; and the forfeiture of any property used to facilitate a violation of federal law, including the Controlled Substances Act.

I hope this letter provides the clarification you have requested, and assists the State of Colorado and its potential licensees in making informed decisions regarding the cultivation, manufacture, and distribution of marijuana, as well as related financial transactions.

Very truly yours,

JOHN F. WALSH
United States Attorney
District of Colorado

cc: Eric Holder, Attorney General of the United States
       James Cole, Deputy Attorney General of the United States

The following memorandum is from the Deputy U.S. Attorney General James M. Cole.

June 29, 2011

MEMORANDUM FOR UNITED STATES ATTORNEYS
FROM: James M. Cole Deputy Attorney General

SUBJECT: Guidance Regarding the Ogden Memo in Jurisdictions Seeking to Authorize Marijuana for Medical Use

"Over the last several months some of you have requested the Department's assistance in responding to inquiries from State and local governments seeking guidance about the Department's position on enforcement of the Controlled Substances Act (CSA) in jurisdictions that have under consideration, or have implemented, legislation that would sanction and regulate the commercial cultivation and distribution of marijuana purportedly for medical use. Some of these jurisdictions have considered approving the cultivation of large quantities of marijuana, or broadening the regulation and taxation of the substance. You may have seen letters responding to these inquiries by several United States Attorneys. Those letters are entirely consistent with the October 2009 memorandum issued by Deputy Attorney General David Ogden to federal prosecutors in States that have enacted laws authorizing the medical use of marijuana (the "Ogden Memo").

The Department of Justice is committed to the enforcement of the Controlled Substances Act in all States. Congress has determined that marijuana is a dangerous drug and that the illegal distribution and sale of marijuana is a serious crime that provides a significant source of revenue to large scale criminal enterprises, gangs, and cartels. The Ogden Memorandum provides guidance to you in deploying your resources to enforce the CSA as part of the exercise of the broad discretion you are given to address federal criminal matters within your districts.

A number of states have enacted some form of legislation relating to the medical use of marijuana. Accordingly, the Ogden Memo reiterated to you that prosecution of significant traffickers of illegal drugs, including marijuana, remains a core priority, but advised that it is likely not an efficient use of federal resources to focus enforcement efforts on individuals with cancer or other serious illnesses who use marijuana as part of a recommended treatment regimen consistent with applicable state law, or their caregivers. The term "caregiver" as used in the memorandum meant just that: individuals providing care to individuals with cancer or other serious illnesses, not commercial operations cultivating, selling or distributing marijuana.

The Department's view of the efficient use of limited federal resources as articulated in the Ogden Memorandum has not changed. There has, however, been an increase in the scope of commercial cultivation, sale, distribution and use of marijuana for purported medical purposes. For example, within the past 12 months, several jurisdictions have considered or enacted legislation to authorize multiple large-scale, privately-operated industrial marijuana cultivation centers. Some of these planned facilities have revenue projections of millions of dollars based on the planned cultivation of tens of thousands of cannabis plants.

The Ogden Memorandum was never intended to shield such activities from federal enforcement action and prosecution, even where those activities purport to comply with state law. Persons who are in the business of cultivating, selling or distributing marijuana, and those who knowingly facilitate such activities, are in violation of the Controlled Substances Act, regardless of state law. Consistent with resource constraints and the discretion you may exercise in your district, such persons are subject to federal enforcement action, including potential prosecution. State laws or local ordinances are not a defense to civil or criminal enforcement of federal law with respect to such conduct, including enforcement of the CSA. Those who engage in transactions involving the proceeds of such activity may also be in violation of federal money laundering statutes and other federal financial laws.

The Department of Justice is tasked with enforcing existing federal criminal laws in all states, and enforcement of the CSA has long been and remains a core priority."

cc: Lanny A. Breuer Assistant Attorney General, Criminal Division
B. Todd Jones United States Attorney District of Minnesota Chair, AGAC
Michele M. Leonhart Administrator Drug Enforcement Administration
H. Marshall Jarrett Director Executive Office for United States Attorneys
Kevin L. Perkins Assistant Director Criminal Investigative Division
Federal Bureau of Investigations

On August 1, 2011, an attorney, David G. Evans, Esq. from Flemington, New Jersey, prepared an excellent opinion on the question: "What are the federal criminal and civil and other liabilities of 'medical' marijuana dispensaries and physicians, government employees, landlords and financiers, who participate in any way in the growing, possession, manufacture, distribution, or sales of medical marijuana under sate 'medical' marijuana laws?"

I would encourage you to get a copy of his legal memorandum or you can read it online at *http://www.concernedfccitizens.org/images/stories/CSAMEMOAUGUST12011.pdf*, at the time of this publication.

The election was just a few days away, and we were feverishly getting reports an updates, wondering where we stood thus far. This is an example of some of our updates that James and Nancy Patella worked on.

Update from county received this morning that covers through end of business yesterday (10/31/11).

This biggest news is that even though Scott Doyle predicted 30% to 33% turnout countywide, the city turnout is 39%, and that doesn't include today.

Only change from voter demographics is the 45 to 59 age group grew from 28% to 30%

This was at the expense of the following age groups:

60 to 74 dropped from 28% to 27%
75 to 89 dropped from 13% to 12%
18 to 29 age group is still at 12%

The actual numbers for voter turnout (except for the 18 to 29 crowd which was kept at 50% to account for the threatened last minute march to turn in ballots) are plugged into the spreadsheet below. Note the below numbers assume a march of almost 5,000 kids. Again, these numbers are as of COB 10/31/11.

I am cautiously optimistic seeing these figures. The following are the cautionary notes:

Can we count on the older demographic voting 60% for us (as did the entire city of Loveland)? We could even tolerate a smaller majority if the younger demographic doesn't turnout as strong as threatened.

Is the 30 to 44 demographic not "old enough" to vote our way? Their turnout rate is well below the older age groups which may help us if not.

Age Group	FC Voter Ballots Mailed	Turnout	Qty Voters	For 300 (%)	For 300 (Qty votes)	Against 300 (Qty votes)
18 to 29	16,519	50%	8,260	30%	2,478	5,782
30 to 44	18,919	27%	5,108	60%	3,065	2,043
45 to 59	18,863	44%	8,300	60%	4,980	3,320
60 to 74	11,711	64%	7,495	60%	4,497	2,998
75 to 89	4,426	73%	3,231	60%	1,939	1,292
90+	578	59%	341	60%	205	136
Total	71,016		32,734		17,163	15,572
					52.43%	47.57%

The chart was prepared by Jim Patella, member of the Concerned Fort Collins Citizens

The October 11, 2011, e-mail was disturbing:

> "Please see http://www.fcgov.com/cityclerk/reports-2011nov. php for the campaign reports of the two issue committees that are competing against us. Talk about David and Goliath. The local issue committee against us has been funded with 6x the amount of money we have collected. It is all coming from the MMDs. Union money is coming in big for the issue committee in Denver. The Denver issue committee has been funded by the union with 70% more money than we collected."

The grocery union from Denver, Colorado, decided to join the efforts of supporting the MMD-industry campaign known as Citizens for Safer Neighborhoods, which is a clever play on words for a title of an organization that I feel is doing contrary to building safer neighborhoods. Seven Fort Collins dispensaries voted to join UFCW Local 7. This was reported in the *Denver Post* on October 18, 2011, just before the November election.

Seriously? Why on earth would a grocery union decide to join forces? This became evident that greed and money was involved, not the care for the ailing community that were seeking medical assistance. The union claimed that they cared about the ill. Where were they in 2000 when Amendment 20 was a hot topic? Where was their care and concern for the ailing people then? Now all of a sudden, their heartfelt compassion a couple of weeks before the election, eleven years later?

Our committee really believed this could be a turning point in the campaign, for the better! Citizens were outraged that an out-of-town organization wanted to tell Fort Collins voters how they should live in a community that the union was not residing. To make things worse, Citizens for Safer Neighborhoods held a fundraising in Denver at the Industry Lounge, 2046 Arapahoe Street, not in Fort Collins. All of a sudden, we started receiving more donations.

We also knew that regardless of the vote turnout, patients will still have access as they have for the last fifty years, but the law now allows patients some protection without the illegal MJ shops. I am convinced we were more concerned for the patients than the illegal marijuana shop owners were; there concern was money. Even during the campaign, all they could talk about was how much sales-tax money the city would lose and how much it would cost them.

During this campaign, council member, Dr. Wade Troxell, stood alone on this battlefront. The current city council, during this campaign, really disappointed a lot of voters. Of all people, I would have thought that Mayor Pro Tem Kelley Ohlsen would have reconsidered the dangers of the MMDs, considering his next-door neighbor was in a gun battle over the MMD issue. His neighbors admitted that the reason why they moved to Colorado was so they could setup a storefront to deliver marijuana out of state. To Kelley's credit, I know he does believe in standing for what the voters say. Also, the council as a whole did work diligently to properly zone the MMDs sites. The mistake was grandfathering the existent MMDs where they were currently located, which meant only two of the twenty-two MMDs would be legally in the newly zoned area.

Nevertheless, this vote should have never gone to the voters. The law was clear that federal law supersedes local and state law; the council knew that this was a clear violation of the law to allow MMDs, and they should have axed the whole matter on the bench by declaring the stores illegal by shutting them down themselves. Instead, it cost the taxpayers over $60,000 to hold the election, because they did not have the intestinal fortitude to make the right decision. The council tried to hide behind the curtain of confusion, claiming that the law was not clear. The law was clear, but the message they delivered for an excuse was not clear. There is an old saying by Prof. Hendricks who *used* to say, "If there's a mist in the pulpit, there's a fog in the pew."

The passion and concern for our community and youth never ceased to amaze me. I remember Dr. Nancy Smith writing me an e-mail note, stating, *"I do believe we each have answered a call to give of our talents, energy, sleepless nights, experience in order to truly protect the future of our youth and our city. When I was a young therapist during the mid-seventies, I was heartbroken by the number of college age/young adults who tragically dulled their brains, became so addicted, and, even when they got sober if they did not, had so damaged themselves they could never become the person they were created to be.*

The loss of one youth's potential is a tragic loss to that individual, his family, and the community at large, and as you know, those lost souls often become a never-ending burden to those that love them and society as a whole . . ."

Question 300 was placed on the ballot to *ban* medical marijuana dispensaries (MMDs). When Colorado voters, out of compassion, voted to allow under state law small quantities of this controlled substance back in 2000, the intent was to reduce the criminal consequences of minor marijuana possession for seriously ill patients. The intent was *never* to distribute mass quantities of marijuana from easy access storefronts across the state. In fact, all dispensing of marijuana continues to be illegal under federal law. What is interesting is that patients got along fine for decades with the help of caregivers and without the MMD stores. What we did in 2000 is just say that what was happening for decades between patients and caregivers would no longer be a crime and subject to prosecution. That is all we said, and that is the last time the citizens had the opportunity to vote.

Back in 2000, the voters were given a blue book that explains the pros and cons of both sides of the issues and clearly states what the ballot issue and law means. Below are sections from the blue book that all voters understood, and it explains the purpose of the blue book.

COLORADO GENERAL ASSEMBLY

EXECUTIVE COMMITTEE
Rep. Russell George, Chairman
Sen. Ray Powers, Vice Chairman
Sen. Tom Blickensderfer
Sen. Michael Feeley
Rep. Doug Dean
Rep. Ken Gordon

STAFF
Charles S. Brown, Director
Daniel Chapman, Assistant Director, Administration
Deborah Godshall, Assistant

COMMITTEE
Sen. Ken Chlouber
Sen. Gigi Dennis
Sen. Rob Hernandez
Sen. Doug Lamborn
Sen. Pat Pascoe
Sen. Bill Thiebaut
Rep. Bob Bacon
Rep. Dorothy Gotlieb
Rep. Steve Johnson
Rep. Shawn Mitchell
Rep. Lola Spradley
Rep. Abel Tapia

LEGISLATIVE COUNCIL
ROOM 029 STATE CAPITOL
DENVER, COLORADO 80203-1784
Email: lcs.ga@state.co.us
(303) 866-3521   FAX: 866-3855   TDD: 866-3472

September 11, 2000

Dear Colorado Voter:

This booklet provides information on proposed changes to the state constitution and state statutes to be decided upon at the 2000 statewide election. The booklet is divided into two sections.

Section 1: Analyses of Proposed Changes to the Colorado Constitution and Statutes
An analysis of each proposed change to the state constitution and state statutes is contained in Section 1. The state constitution requires the nonpartisan research staff of the General Assembly to prepare these analyses and to distribute them in a ballot information booklet to active registered voters. Each analysis describes the major provisions of a proposal and comments on the proposal's application and effect. Major arguments are summarized for and against each measure. Careful consideration has been given to the arguments in an effort to fairly represent both sides of the issue. The Legislative Council, the committee of the General Assembly responsible for reviewing the analyses, takes no position with respect to the merits of the proposals.

Section 2: Title and Text of Proposed Referred and Initiated Measures
The title and the legal language of each proposed change to the state constitution and state statutes is printed in Section 2 of the booklet

Sincerely

Russell George

Representative Russell George
Chairman

ANALYSES

AMENDMENT 20
MEDICAL USE OF MARIJUANA

The proposed amendment to the Colorado Constitution:

◆ allows patients diagnosed with a serious or chronic illness and their care-givers to legally possess marijuana for medical purposes. For a patient unable to administer marijuana to himself or herself, or for minors under 18, care-givers determine the amount and frequency of use;

♦ allows a doctor to legally provide a seriously or chronically ill patient with a written statement that the patient might benefit from medical use of marijuana; and

♦ establishes a confidential state registry of patients and their care-givers who are permitted to possess marijuana for medical purposes.

Background and Provisions of the Proposal

Current Colorado and federal criminal law prohibits the possession, distribution, and use of marijuana. The proposal does not affect federal criminal laws, but amends the Colorado Constitution to legalize the medical use of marijuana for patients who have registered with the state. Qualifying medical conditions include cancer, glaucoma, AIDS/HIV, some neurological and movement disorders such as multiple sclerosis, and any other medical condition approved by the state. A doctor's signed statement or a copy of the patient's pertinent medical records indicating that the patient might benefit from marijuana is necessary for a patient to register. Individuals on the registry may possess up to two ounces of usable marijuana and six marijuana plants. Because the proposal does not change current law, distribution of marijuana will still be illegal in Colorado.

Patients on the registry are allowed to legally acquire, possess, use, grow, and transport marijuana and marijuana paraphernalia. Employers are not required to allow the medical use of marijuana in the workplace. Marijuana may not be used in any place open to the public, and insurance companies are not required to reimburse a patient's claim for costs incurred through the medical use of marijuana. Finally, for a patient who is under the age of 18, the proposal requires statements from two doctors and written consent from any parent living in Colorado to register the patient.

1) Using marijuana is not necessary to relieve nausea, increase appetite, and alleviate pain. Many other prescription drugs, including Marinol, which contains a synthetic version of THC, are currently available. Further, this proposal sets a dangerous precedent for approval and regulation of medicines by popular vote. It circumvents the usual rigorous process by which all other medicines are legalized and regulated. Safe and effective medicines should be developed through scientific and reproducible research. 2) The proposal does not provide any legal means by which a patient may obtain marijuana. Under state criminal law, it will still be illegal to sell marijuana or marijuana plants to another individual, including a patient on the state registry. Under federal criminal law, it will continue to be illegal to sell or use marijuana for any purpose.

Chapter 5 Endnotes

1. U.S. Attorney General, District of Colorado, John Walsh memo to Colorado Attorney General, John Suthers, April 26, 2011, *http://www. concernedfccitizens.org/images/stories/US%20Atty%20Walsh%20 Letter%20Med%20MJ.pdf*, accessed March 14, 2012
2. MEMORANDUM FOR UNITED STATES ATTORNEYS, FROM: James M. Cole Deputy Attorney General, June 29, 2011, *http://www. concernedfccitizens.org/images/stories/Cole%20Memo.pdf*, accessed March 14, 2012
3. On August 1, 2011, an attorney, David G. Evans, Esq. from Flemington, New Jersey, legal memorandum online at *http://www.concernedfccitizens. org/images/stories/CSAMEMOAUGUST12011.pdf*, at the time of this publication, accessed March 14, 2012
4. *Two more marijuana initiatives filed—Denver Post*, *http://www. denverpost.com/breakingnews/ci_20167843/two-more-marijuana- initiatives-filed?IADID=Search-www.denverpost.com-www.denverpost. com#ixzz1q0Xk9nh1*, accessed March 23, 2012

CHAPTER 6

The Law of the Land

On February 9, 2012, several of us on the committee to oppose the marijuana stores were subpoenaed to district court in Larimer County where the Honorable Thomas French, judge of the district court for the Eighth Judicial District, presided in courtroom 5(C), to hear the case regarding the constitutional right of medical marijuana store closures.

During the November 2011 election, the ballot measure 300 won approval of the people to close all medical marijuana dispensaries (MMD) within the City of Fort Collins, Colorado. The stores had to close by February 14, 2012, which was more than ample time for the MMDs to close. However, a week before the court hearing on February 9, a Denver attorney filed a lawsuit claim on behalf of several MMD stores, declaring monetary damages and questioning the constitutionality of the voters being able to close the stores.

The plaintiffs were named as "Medicinal Gardens of Colorado, Inc., a Colorado corporation, d/b/a "Medicinal Gardens," et al., and the defendants were named as the City of Fort Collins, a Colorado Home Rule Municipal Corporation, et al.

The attorney for the plaintiffs was Brett S. Barney, and named defendants were Sheriff Justin Smith and Larry Abrahamson, City of Fort Collins, and the Colorado Department of Revenue. The attorneys, Kraig Ekton and Corey Hoffmann, for the City of Fort Collins did an excellent job in defending the rights of the voters. The other attorneys for the state and the county were present to protect their best interests as well.

I am amazed how unprepared the Denver attorney was in his case before the court. There was not any organization on his part. He did not prepare his own witnesses for testimony, and they obviously did not know what he was going to ask them. Several of his witnesses (store owners) admitted that they knew selling marijuana was illegal. Well, that in itself causes the MMDs to lose their case.

This battle for the rights of the voters through our committee was on several fronts.

1. We had to petition at least 4,200 registered voters' signatures.
2. The campaign was an uphill battle to raise money and get our message out. The MMD stores raised over $110,000 to our $14,000, yet the people were able to see through the deception of the MMD store owners.
3. After winning the election, city council considered approving another method of allowing marijuana stores to continue their sales under the guise of caregivers, which we were able to secure a unanimous decision to not allow the ordinance to pass.
4. Then the court case before Judge French trying to accuse committee members, the City of Fort Collins, and the district attorney's office of violating their constitutional rights.

I think you will find that the judge's ruling was very clear and articulated the facts and what the law states:

> *"THE COURT: I' m going to cut to the chase on this. It seems cruel and perverse to wait until 15 or 20 minutes to explain my reason before I give you my results, so I' m going to give you the ruling, then I' m going to tell you why I have concluded that way. So the Court denies the request for temporary restraining order and preliminary injunction or the ground that neither the preliminary threshold requirements are met for a preliminary injunction and none of the five factors under Rathke v. McFarlane, M—c—F—a—r—l—a—n—e, 6 4 8 P.2 d 6 4 8, were met. So let me tell you the rational for the ruling. Plaintiffs filed a verified complaint and application for declaratory and injunctive relief on January 26, 2012, some months after the election which led to the initiated ordinance*

being passed. Plaintiffs filed the motion for temporary restraining order and show cause for preliminary injunction on February 26, 2012. In the original verified complaint, plaintiffs have six grounds for relief. However, the Court is only hearing the temporary restraining order and request for preliminary injunctive relief a t this time.

As such, the Court is hearing the issue on the plaintiffs' request to enjoy enforcement of the initiated ordinance, their request to enjoin actions on plaintiffs' licenses, their request to enjoin shutting down of plaintiffs' businesses based on the initiated ordinance, and their request to enjoin harassment of plaintiffs; and finally, their request to enjoin alleged interference with plaintiffs' right to contract.

The request for declaratory relief made by plaintiffs are not yet ripe for determination.

Plaintiffs are businesses and business owners of medical marijuana centers, and they have licenses concerning optional premises cultivation or medical marijuana—infused product manufacturing.

The gravamen of plaintiffs' complaint are that the City of Fort Collins seeks to improperly cause their businesses to cease and desist any business activities related to medical marijuana centers, optional premises cultivation or medical marijuana-infused product manufacturing by midnight of February 14, 2012.

The Court heard evidence today, February 9, 2012, from plaintiffs' witnesses, considered exhibits admitted, reviewed the pleadings, considered the briefs by the parties, considered the applicable law and heard argument.

Based upon that, the Court finds as follows:

Rathke v. MacFarlane is the seminal Colorado case on the granting of injunctive relief. In pertinent part, the Supreme

Court stated as follows in that case, quote, We conclude that before a trial court may enjoin the enforcement of a criminal statute in a preliminary injunction proceeding, moving party must establish, as a threshold requirement, a clear showing that injunctive relief is necessary to protect existing legitimate property rights or fundamental constitutional rights. That's at 64 8 P. 2d—I have the Lexis Nexis version; that's page 7.

In this case, Colorado Constitutional Amendment—what is referred to as Amendment No. 20 to the Colorado Constitution provides a limited exception to criminal liability for possession, distribution or sale of marijuana, provides a limited affirmative defense to those charged with possession or distribution of marijuana.

Stated recently in the case of People v. Watkins, 2012 COA 15, dated February 2nd of this year, quote, The amendment (20) provides, It shall be an exception from the State's criminal laws for any patient in lawful possession of a, quote, registry identification card to use marijuana for medicinal purposes. Skipping a ways down, same opinion: While possession of marijuana remains a criminal offense in Colorado, Section 18-18-4 06 (1) CRS 2 0 11, a patient's medical use of marijuana within the limits set forth in the Amendment is deemed lawful in Section (4) (a) of the Amendment.

And then skipping down further in the same opinion, As a division of this court recognized in Beinor, the Amendment created a defense to civil prosecution and is not a—this is a quote within a quote—grant to medical marijuana users of an unlimited constitutional right to use the drug in any place or any manner, end of quote, end of entire quote as well.

Possession, sale or distribution of any amount of marijuana even if it's for medical purposes is a crime under federal law. That federal law is directly applicable to the States. That is also from the recent case of People v. Watkins.

As such, plaintiffs can be arrested for the sale or distribution of marijuana under federal law and business confiscated under federal laws a t anytime. The federal government is still prosecuting in Colorado for possession, sale or distribution of marijuana.

The Court finds the plaintiffs do not logically or legally claim a fundamental constitutional right in an activity that is illegal under federal law. How limited is this exception under Colorado law? Well, it does not allow or provide marijuana patients the right to access a particular source, right to access the most convenient source of marijuana, or right to access the closest source of marijuana, nor does it allow sellers the right to purchase or sell in the city of their residence, or a right to purchase or sell in the city of their choice.

All of the witnesses—plaintiff party witnesses in this case were asked the question, acknowledged that they knew that the sale of marijuana was not legal under federal law when they started—I believe six of the plaintiffs who were the six who were asked that question—Mr. Ackerman, I do not believe, was asked that question. The other plaintiffs were asked that question. They agreed that they knew it was not legal under federal law to sell or possess marijuana when they started their businesses.

Plaintiffs allege that their First Amendment rights have been silenced by the ordinance on its face. Upon deeper examination, the initiated ordinance does not silence or limit plaintiffs' First Amendment rights.

The initiated ordinance in question seeks to prohibit—or does prohibit, rather, the operation of medical marijuana—this is a quote, the operation of medical marijuana centers, optional premises cultivation operations and medical marijuana-infused products manufacturing within the City of Fort Collins, end of quote.

The plaintiffs claim that this ordinance is unconstitutional and an unconstitutional burden on their free speech rights because their, quote, operations include educational and political activity. They allege that the ordinance amounts to prohibition of these activities.

However, it appears clear to the Court that the ordinance, quote, does not implicate the First Amendment because it was directed at conduct, not speech, end of quote.

That quote is from People v. Shell, 148 P.3d 162(Colo. 2006), Shell spelled S-h-e-l-l. In Shell, the Supreme Court of Colorado held that a ban on the unauthorized practice of law did not violate freedom of speech. The Court reasoned that, quote, The fact that our ban touches on the legal content of the advice offered or the pleadings drafted by an unlicensed person is of no constitutional significance since, quote—single quote—it has never been deemed an abridgement of freedom of speech or press to make a course of conduct illegal merely because the conduct was in part initiated, evidenced, or carried out by means of language, either spoken, written, or printed, end of quote.

Here, a medical marijuana center is defined as a, quote, business that sells medical marijuana to registered patients or primary caregivers.

An optional premises cultivation operation is a licensed business that is authorized to grow and cultivate marijuana. A medical marijuana—infused marijuana is a person licensed to operate a business that makes products infused with medical marijuana intended for use or consumption or by smoking; thus, the ordinance, reasonably interpreted, merely prohibits selling, growing, cultivating or infusing other products within marijuana in Fort Collins.

The general assembly presumably delegated the authority to prohibit these operations to the City of Fort Collins. The ordinance in plain language is not prohibiting education of

*the public about the benefits alleged of medical marijuana,
nor does it prohibit or is aimed at reforming Colorado's drug
law.*

*Plaintiffs' constitutional use is as centers as a gathering
place and forum where people can discuss ideas and obtain
information. They just cannot also sell or grow marijuana.
Only by actively selling or cultivating marijuana can the
plaintiffs violate the ordinance.*

Therefore, plaintiffs' First Amendment claims must fall.

*Plaintiffs also assert property rights in their licenses to sell
marijuana, to grow it and to make marijuana-infused products.
However, it's clear under the statute that application fees,
quote, shall not equate to a local or state license or present or
future time to receive a license, end of quote. That's a quote
from the statute.*

*There is no constitutional-protected right to conduct a business
that may be prohibited in the exercise of police powers of the
state.*

*Plaintiffs assert they have a property right because of the
Colorado Medical Marijuana Code. The Court disagrees.
Under Colorado law, the legal interest conveyed or created by
a license is merely a personal privilege to do some particular
act or series of acts. An ordinary license is revocable at the
will of the licensor. That's from Patzer v. Loveland, 80 P.3d
908 (Colo. App. 2003). Ms. Tucker I believe said it well. She
said in business, nothing is for certain. That was her testimony
here today.*

*Personal privilege is an irrevocable license that is renewable
within the sound discretion of the licensing official who can
be reached by proceedings in the event of arbitrary abuse of
that discretion is not proper in the constitutional sense and
no vested rights are acquired when it is obtained under the*

authority of City and County v. Trailkill, T-r-a-i-l-k-i-l-l, 244 P.2d 1074 (Colo. 1952.)

Along the same lines, commonly said, a vested right must be something more than a mere expectation based upon anticipated continuance of the existing law, Ficarra v. department of Regulatory Agencies, 849 P.2d 6 (Colo. 1993).

In addition, plaintiffs cannot establish that they are entitled to continue operating their businesses or have a vested right to operate their businesses under 12-43.3-103 of the Colorado Medical Marijuana Code. That section of the code provides, among other things, as follows: That a person—let me cut to the chase here, basically, this is (1) (a) of that statute, says, a person who is operating a locally approved business may do so—may operate that business in accordance with any local laws.

And later on in that statute, paragraph (1)(b), it says, Payment of the fee and completion of the form shall not create a local or state license or a present or future entitlement to receive a license. And that is commonly referred to as the local option or local opt-out statute, which is 12-43.3-106, reads as follows—I'm going to read this chapter just so that I can reliably interpret the document, the pertinent part, quote, The operation of this article shall be statewide unless a municipality, county, city, or city and county, by either a majority of registered electors of the municipality, county, city, or city and county voting at a regular selection or special election vote to prohibit the operation of medical marijuana centers, optional premises cultivation operations, and medical marijuana-infused products manufacturers' licenses.

So the Court finds that the plaintiffs do not have a property interest that can be—that should be protected to the extent required under Rathke. So the Court finds that plaintiffs have not met the threshold requirement for injunctive relief, not made a clear showing that the injunctive relief is necessary to protect fundamental constitutional rights or existing property rights.

Assuming, arguendo, that those threshold requirements had been met, which they have not, even under the rest of the Rathke analysis, plaintiffs are not entitled to the requested injunctive relief.

Here's what Rathke says, second part of opinion: However, injunctive relief should not be indiscriminately granted. Crosby v. Watson, supra. Rather, it should be exercised sparingly and cautiously and with a full conviction on the part of the trial court of its urgent necessity.

Therefore, once the trial court has determined that the threshold requirement has been met for the issuance of a preliminary injunction to enjoin the enforcement of a criminal statute, it must then determine whether the moving party has established the prerequisites for preliminary injunctive relief, C.R.C.P. 65(a).

In exercising its discretion, the trial court must find that the moving party has demonstrated—then it lists the six factors for injunctive relief.

Number one, the first factor, a reasonable probability of success on the merits.

Plaintiffs challenged the constitutionality of the initiated ordinance and portions of the Colorado Medical Marijuana Code. Their burden is to prove beyond a reasonable doubt that the statutes are unconstitutional, and the Court is presuming that the statutes are constitutional. The Court does so.

And when the Court does so, it finds no compelling argument has been advanced that the initiated ordinance or House Bill 1284 is unconstitutional. So the Court finds that there is no reasonable probability of success on the merits.

The second factor under Rathke, A danger of real, immediate, and irreparable injury which may be prevented by injunctive relief. In this case, the plaintiffs allege that the real, immediate, and irreparable injury is that their businesses will be closed down on February 14th if the injunctive relief requested is not provided.

However, the Court finds that even if that occurs, the damages will not be irreparable, because they can be compensated by money damages. Loss of money is not irreparable injury under American Investors Life Insurance v. Green Shield Plan, 358 P.2d 343 (Colo. 1961).

The third factor under Rathke is that there is no plain, speedy, and adequate remedy at law. The Court finds that there is a plain, speedy and adequate remedy. That's what this case is about. Based upon the testimony of the plaintiffs in this case, that is what it's about.

Moreover, plaintiffs are concurrently seeking declaratory relief, and such relief can also be an adequate remedy at law.

The fourth factor under Rathke is whether the preliminary injunction disserves the public interests. And stated more clearly, that fourth factor is, quote, that the granting of a preliminary injunction will not disserve the public interests.

So the question is whether the granting the public—whether the preliminary injunctive relief will disserve the public interests. The public interests and voice has been demonstrated by the result of the election in this case.

The people—the constituency of voters voted to ban the items indicated in the initiated ordinance. I think that the public has spoken on that particular issue in regard to state statutes governing the sale of marijuana; the general assembly, which already decided that compliance with House Bill 1284 is in the public interests, and they have stated that the statute is an exercise of the State's police power for the protection of economic and social welfare and the health, peace and morals of the people in our state.

The final factor under Rathke is the balance of—whether the balance of the equities favor the injunction—I'm not—the next-to-last factor—favors the injunction.

The Court finds that the plaintiffs' equities do not favor the injunction because plaintiffs can obtain money damages, can take their businesses elsewhere. And the citizens have expressed their will in this case. Finally, the sixth factor is whether the injunction will preserve the status quo pending a trial on the merits.

The first question is, what is the status quo, the status quo before the election or since the election? The Court finds that the status quo today is that plaintiffs can sell marijuana in compliance with their licenses, but only do so until February 14, 2012. The Court finds that is the status quo. That is because that is the date when the prohibition goes into effect. This ruling does not disturb that situation, that status quo.

So the Court finds that none of the six factors under Rathke have been granted here. As stated before, the Court does not find that either of the preliminary threshold requirements necessary for preliminary injunctive relief in this situation have been met, so the Court denies the request for the temporary restraining order and preliminary injunction.

Procedural questions.

Mr. Barney, anything?

MR. BARNEY: I guess there's nothing else to say, Your Honor.

THE COURT: Thank you. On behalf of the defendants in this matter?

MR. HOFFMANN: Nothing from the Fort Collins defendants, Your Honor.

THE COURT: That concludes this matter. The Court is adjourned until 8:30 tomorrow morning. Thank you."

(The proceedings were adjourned at the hour of 4:41 p.m.)

REPORTER'S CERTIFICATE

I, Debbie Zoetewey, an Official Court Reporter in and for the Eighth Judicial District of the State of Colorado, do hereby certify that the foregoing transcript is a full, true, and complete transcription of my stenotype notes taken in my capacity as Official Reporter at the time and place above set forth.

Dated this 23rd day of February, 2012, in Fort Collins, Larimer County, Colorado.

/s/ Debbie Zoetewey
Debbie Zoetewey, CSR, RMR

CHAPTER 7

Public Letters for the Media Opposing MMDs

The following is a public letter I wrote regarding the vote on ballot 300 in the City of Fort Collins, Colorado:

"City Council voted to allow us to decide if we want marijuana distribution centers in Fort Collins; this was never voted on before by the people. In fact, it was decided in 2009, by unelected officials who overturned your vote, thus departing from Amendment 20, and allowing marijuana storefronts.

"In 2000, Colorado voters approved Amendment 20 to allow medical marijuana. The amendment doesn't allow distribution through dispensaries. Since that decision to allow marijuana storefronts, parents, schools, substance abuse treatment providers, and police officials have experienced negative effects plaguing our youth and community. The Sheriff reported an increase of marijuana related crimes up by 20% in the county, and a 40% increase in the City.

"Amendment 20 is intended to provide a compassionate approach that balances the legitimate needs of the seriously ill and debilitated patient who only finds relief through marijuana; this law takes the crime out of possessing small quantities for individuals or care-giver grown marijuana. The storefronts violate the voters' intent. Council zoned where these stores could operate, but grandfathered all of them in that were outside the designated zone. Consequently, only 2 of the 21 stores are zoned correctly—overriding almost all restrictions on proximity to schools, daycare centers, etc.

"Regardless, the voters must consider whether the distribution of marijuana is even legal, which the state and federal law is clear about being illegal, and whether we want the storefronts. Remember, "professional guidance" is given by doctors, not marijuana store clerks.""

On September 18, 2002, the *New York Times* printed as the following as a full-page ad, "An Open Letter to Parents about Marijuana."

"Marijuana puts kids at risk. It is the most widely used illicit drug among youth today and is more potent than ever. Marijuana use can lead to a host of significant health, social, learning, and behavioral problems at a crucial time in a young person's development . . . Kids can get hooked on pot . . . More teens enter treatment for marijuana abuse each year than for all other illicit drugs combined."

The ad was signed by eighteen organizations. Among them are American Academy of Family Physicians, American Academy of Pediatrics, American College of Emergency Physicians, American Medical Association, American Society of Addiction Medicine, Child Welfare League of America, National Center for School Health Nursing, National Medical Association, and the National Parent Teachers Association.

I care about the seriously ill, and I also care about the health of our youth. We cannot afford the social cost and ramifications of our young adults' future by closing our eyes to the truth being undermined. Next we will see other habit-forming drugs being considered as medicine through popular votes instead of the FDA.

The heavy marketing that you see today is only the beginning. We never see doctors and pharmacists doing sign dancing on our streets promoting drugs. Pharmacies don't entice a person to take drugs through tantalizing candy wrappers that simulate other popular brands of candy. The intent is wrong, and it is up to us to correct it and bring out the truth.

Sheriff's Office seizure after arrests for armed robbery
of MMD store in Fort Collins.

Picture courtesy of the Larimer County Sheriff's Office

I was on the board of director for Concerned Citizens of Fort Collins when we approved submitting the following letter to the Fort Collins City Council. Keep in mind, one of our board members was City Council Member Wade Troxell, whom I admire for taking a stance, even though the rest of council were hiding behind a political curtain.

CONCERNED FORT COLLINS CITIZENS

August 8, 2011

City Council
City of Fort Collins
300 W. Laporte Ave.
Fort Collins, CO 80521

Dear City Councilors,

Let us begin by expressing our sincere gratitude to Council Members who are dealing with this contentious issue of marijuana store fronts for a long time, and to those who are entering the community debate for the first time. The initiation and success of the petition was not done out of an effort to blame Council members who cast deciding votes to maintain the commercial marijuana industry in Fort Collins. Each of you made your decision based on the understood information before you; and for that we are not critical.

Our petition campaign was launched because we don't believe that the decision did not accurately reflect the deeply held values of a majority of Fort Collins citizens. We also believe that some information and perspectives that we hope to bring to you in the Council meeting on August 16 were not available to you in the discernment process of your earlier decisions.

The petition being presented to you on August 16 was initiated out of a desire to let the citizens speak. The purpose was to ask City Council to conduct a special election in November 2011, allowing citizens the opportunity to vote to close or keep medical marijuana dispensaries, commercial grow operations, and infused product manufacturing in Fort Collins. The proposed ordinance in the petition gives City Council two choices—to refer the ordinance to the voters, or, by Council decision, to adopt the ordinance as is without incurring the expense and time of a Special Election.

We are people of compassion and acknowledge the Colorado Constitutional law known as Amendment 20, adopted in November 2000. There are citizens in Fort Collins who suffer from legitimate serious debilitating illnesses, some under the care of legitimate caregivers giving significant guidance to the debilitated patient.

Our deeply held belief is the commercial medical marijuana industry that exists in Fort Collins today is not consistent with *voter intent* in the adoption of Amendment 20, but essentially de-facto legalization of the recreational use of marijuana. Voter intent on each statewide ballot issue is formed by the information provided prior to each election by the State Legislature in the *Voter Blue Book*. We have attached the *Voter Blue Book* language given to voters prior to their vote to adopt Amendment 20. The intent clearly states that Amendment 20 is to de-criminalize the possession of limited quantities of marijuana in the possession of legitimate debilitated patients and their caregivers and medical doctors who are giving significant care. Distribution systems were not prescribed in Amendment 20, and it is clear that any distribution and sale of marijuana for medical purposes *would remain illegal under state law*.

In October 2009, U.S. Deputy Attorney General Ogden, issued a memo (the Ogden Memo) that states no federal resources will not be to prosecute patients and caregivers in possession of marijuana for medical purposes. This memo was very loosely read and interpreted, giving rise in many states to the commercialization of the medical marijuana industry. After launching our petition initiative, several key federal documents were issued stating the deep resolve of the Federal Government to enforce the law regarding marijuana possession and sale.

Since Colorado legalized marijuana for medical purposes in 2000, it has remained a federal law that the possession and sale of marijuana is illegal, as the drug remains on Schedule-I under the Controlled Substances Act (CSA). Included in your packet are several letters/opinions that outline the seriousness of the federal government in clarifying the misconceptions arising from the Ogden Memo; they are seriousness about addressing those violations. It is our hope that by including these documents you will discuss this issue with the City Attorney regarding several contingent points of deep concern to the citizens you represent, and the City employees under your care. These concerns include the following:

a) Are you and sworn City of Fort Collins employees under your care, in violation of your oath of office to uphold the law?

b) From the opinion letter of August 1, 2011 by New Jersey attorney David Evans, it is clear that the federal government is beginning to prosecute violators of the Controlled Substance Act. Could Colorado be the next target?

c) Many Federal grants include a provision that the funding provided must be returned if the entity receiving the money is in violation of Federal law. Could this be an unintended consequence of our current ordinance governing the commercial medical marijuana industry in Fort Collins?

d) The Evans memo states "Because the provisions of the state "medical" marijuana laws that authorize the possession, use, cultivation, and distribution of marijuana are preempted by the CSA, those . . . government employees . . . who act pursuant to the state laws are at risk of violating federal laws." By continuing to allow the commercial medical marijuana industry in Fort Collins, are you placing city employees, and yourselves, in jeopardy through your activities of facilitating and governing the industry in our city?

e) Is it possible to create immunity for yourselves, and city employees, by referring the proposed ordinance to a vote and allowing the voters to decide whether we, as a City, follow federal law or not?

We are sure other questions and concerns will come to mind as you prepare for the discussion on August 16. It is our hope that, in providing this information, you will make a fully informed decision regarding the ordinance contained in the petition initiative—do you adopt now, or refer to the voters for the special election.

We sincerely appreciate the time you are taking to prepare, and to hear both sides presented on August 16.

With Gratitude

Chairperson of the Committee

The following letter was written by the district attorney of the Eighth Judicial District, Larry Abrahamson, that was released to the media:

District Attorney, Eighth Judicial District, 2005-2013,
and over forty years of experience

"In June of last year, I wrote a Soapbox suggesting areas of concern the Fort Collins City Council should consider when debating whether to "opt-out" and prohibit the establishment of marijuana dispensaries in the city. While several towns and cities around Colorado chose to disallow the commercial sale of marijuana, the city council of Fort Collins did not. Many are now asking, is this issue of such magnitude that the effects to our city's image and character should be decided by its citizens?

"We can debate whether a patient has a legitimate debilitating condition that can only be treated by marijuana. We can conjecture as to whether those who need the healing powers of THC will be able to obtain the drug legally. Also, we might speculate that patients who need marijuana or their care givers do not possess the expertise or equipment to grow their own as envisioned by the constitutional amendment. These propositions may or may not be true; however we have no data that will support these claims to the level they are a serious issue.

"However, data does support: Marijuana use among our children has led directly to Poudre School District suspensions that have tripled over the last couple years. We also know that police are reporting an increase in home invasions and criminal activity that has a direct relationship to the availability of marijuana. Further, students are reporting that they often obtain access to marijuana through relatives and friends who have medical marijuana permits. And we know that dispensaries are a clear violation of the federal Controlled Substance Act subjecting owners, landlords and operators of centers to the risk of federal prosecution and personal and real property forfeiture.

"It is true that the state and city have imposed significant regulations on the operation of dispensaries and the city has received significant tax revenues from marijuana sales. However, as a community we must ask if money is the gauge we should use to determine the appropriateness of commercial dispensaries in Fort Collins?

"Regulations are not always enough. As stringent as city and state regulations may be, they cannot impose requirements that dispensed marijuana be tested for harmful pesticides, that the intake strength (now 5-10 times greater than the same drug used in the 60's) be monitored or controlled, that only pharmacies can dispense the product as medicine, or that controlled FDA testing be imposed to determine the effectiveness and quality of the marijuana sold (AMA refuses to endorse medical marijuana for this very reason). Do we suppose that our youth who see marijuana as "medicinal" may become desensitized to the drugs known and proven dangers? Is the presence and acceptance of commercially sold marijuana the image we want for the choice city?

"Perhaps the voters should decide."

Fort Collins Special Investigations Unit conduct major drug raids
for illegal distribution of drugs in the late 1980s.

Permission granted by the *Coloradoan News*; newspaper clipping
—photo by Kent Meireis/*Coloradoan*

I asked Larimer County Sheriff Justin Smith to explain his experience from law enforcement's perspective, which I think you will find astounding. On March 24, 2012, Sheriff Smith prepared the following statement exclusively for this publication:

Colorado, Larimer County Sheriff Smith was sworn into office on
January 11, 2011, and has twenty-five years of law enforcement experience

"When the United States Attorney General hung out the white flag and the State of Colorado began to sanction commercial production and sales of pot, I began to notice what looked like a significant uptrend in marijuana problems in the county.

"Anecdotally, it seemed that more and more often, marijuana-related incidents were appearing in our electronic Tour of Duty (TDR) reports that the shift sergeants file daily. Experience taught me twenty years ago that drugs and alcohol are involved in the vast majority of incidents that are called into us. However, the prevalence of marijuana as a significant factor seemed to be going through the roof. Routinely, deputies noted that DUI arrests involved drivers smoking pot, deputies came across illegal possession of user amounts of pot where the suspect stated it was for medical purposes, but did not have a state card, citizens reported illegal pot grows in their neighborhoods, we experienced home invasion robberies into pot grows or pot dealers homes, people reported being kidnapped and later admitted the "kidnappings" were actually drug rip offs, kids were getting caught possessing pot at schools. The list just went on and on.

"Being a professional law-enforcement executive, it was important to objectively quantify this problem, because perceptions can be inaccurate. I realized that quantifying the problem would be a little difficult, because the strategy of the pot lobby was to muddle the laws so as to discourage cops from enforcing the current laws. This worked to their advantage because when cops quit enforcing the laws, criminal cases would decrease and the pot lobby would and did use this to claim that pot was no longer a problem.

"When the floodgates on pot-possession permits opened, the state was immediately overwhelmed by applications. The state responded by changing the procedures and rules on almost a daily basis. At one point, it got so bad that pot users were told that all they had to do was to fill out an application and send it in and keep a copy of the certified letter that they sent to the state. The cops were told that if a person had even a copy of an envelope, that was a good as a state permit. Can you ever imagine that we treated driver's licenses that way? On the street, we found that users were sending blank envelopes to the state and using that as protection when they were found in illegal possession of pot. Pot growers were only required to have a copy of those certificates on their property and could claim that they were "caretakers" for those users. We found that there were untold numbers of copies of these permits floating around and we essentially had no way of verifying the validity of most of these permits.

"We actually saw other police agencies in our state begin to turn their back on the marijuana violations in their community, sometimes out of frustration with the confusion over the law and other times because their city councils told them to regulate it, so they could collect taxes from it. To further complicate things, the pot lobby began to buy off state legislators and we saw an already weak law further diluted to increase the amount of pot that a person could possess before it even became a misdemeanor offense. Under the revised laws, a suspect had to be caught with a full two ounces (typically two quart-sized bags full) of marijuana in their possession before it could be more that a petty offense, which meant ticket and release. Their strategy had undeniably been effective.

"To capture the full picture of the effect, we queried police records systems to look for cases where marijuana was involved. We knew that possession arrests would be skewed, because the possession laws had just been gutted. It would be like doubling the speed limit on a road, then claiming it was safer because there were fewer speeders.

"We looked at data over the two year period of 2009 to 2010. We suspected the numbers would be up, but we were truly shocked by the results. In the unincorporated area, we saw an increase from 541 incidents in 2009 to 649 in 2010. That was an increase of roughly 20% from one year to another. Even more telling was the data from within the city limits of Fort Collins. In 2009, they had 502 marijuana-related incidents, but by 2010, that had skyrocketed to 714, which was roughly a 40% increase. Even more telling was that when the city was looked at by police patrol districts, the ones nearest the college campus saw significantly higher increases. This was occurring at the same time that overall crime continued a slow and steady downward trend.

"At the same time, the Colorado Department of Transportation released statewide data on marijuana, impaired driver arrests. Statewide, they saw arrests increase from 391 in 2009 to a reported 599 in 2010. That was an increase of 50%.

"In our dealings with the pot growers, we found that they had worked to refine their message and their image drastically from 2009 to 2010. The partylike pot image that they began with was transforming. Their new look was cleaned up. The marijuana leaves on their signs and advertisements were being replaced with green crosses meant to portray the legitimate medical industry. Whenever they appeared at local city council meetings, they paraded a group of individuals who portrayed the image of what Coloradans had voted for with Amendment 20—mature to elderly persons claiming to be suffering from cancer, MS, glaucoma, etc. All would step up to the microphone and tell how they had always opposed legalized marijuana, how they had never used marijuana before being stricken with these debilitating conditions, then stating that marijuana was the only thing that brought them any relief. The funny thing was that in the field, my deputies were not running into these people in possession of pot. We were continually coming across the young and healthy in possession of state pot cards. In the course of their duties, our crime-impact unit spent just a few hours outside two local dispensaries, documenting who the customers of these shops were. Just as expected, the customers were quite young and not showing any signs of the physical ailments that were always touted by the shop owners. We saw carloads of young people pull up and watched as the cardholder went into the store and came out with the "score." We saw young people run, ride their bicycles and motorcycles to the store. Despite the state laws requiring that cardholders be state residents, we saw customers come and go in vehicles from out of state. We contacted one customer on a traffic offense after he left and found that his card didn't designate that business as his caregiver, so we seized his pot and wrote him a pot-possession ticket. Lesson learned? No, he went home, changed clothes, and came right back and bought again! The most ironic result was that we saw a Ft. Collins City employee, in their uniform shirt go into the pot shop, apparently on break to score some weed. This made for a sad picture of our community.

"Despite our objections to concerns about the marketing of this "medicine" as candy, we were assured this wasn't happening in our community. This also proved to be a blatant lie. When one of the city dispensaries was robbed in 2010, my deputies pursued and captured the robbers as they left the city. In the abandoned car was found not only trash bags of marijuana buds, but also edibles from the dispensary. Those edibles included professionally packaged Bad Ass Brownies and Canna Crispies—made with Rice Crispy cereal. These looked just like the products that children might buy at the checkout stand at any local grocery or convenience store. Sadly, if these products showed up in the lunch boxes of students, teachers would have no way of knowing that they were consuming pot right there in the lunchroom. Even further, kids could unknowingly consume these if handed to them by another student.

"As this state-sanctioned industry grew, we also noticed that traditional illegal grows soared in the county as well. Proponents of state-sanctioned pot shops had assured the community that their industry would reduce this "black market." As the Sheriff, I wish this had been true, but it wasn't. Landlords found that renters were moving into their properties, establishing significant grows and leaving the homes dangerous and uninhabitable. The results from these grow operations were strikingly similar to meth labs. Chemicals being used as fertilizers and pesticides were permeating these homes. The high-moisture concentrations from these plants made the mold factories as well. On the advice of the EPA, the DEA, as well as the county health department, we found the protective gear (haz-mat suits and respirators) that we had purchased to safeguard our deputies dismantling drug labs was just as necessary when they entered these grow houses. This irked the pot-industry advocates who were touting the natural, healthy image of the pot-growing industry. The full threat from this is still not fully known. We are awaiting the results of medical studies being conducted as the National Jewish Hospital in Denver identifying the health dangers posed in these grow operations."

Sheriff's Office seizure after arrests for armed robbery
of MMD store in Fort Collins. Notice the marijuana buds around the
THC-eatables enclosed in a container.

Picture courtesy of the Larimer County Sheriff's Office

Fort Collins City Council member, Dr. Wade Troxell, was the only council member that took a public stand against the MMDs and spoke candidly about the truths and image that he did not want Fort Collins to have, beings the city has many excellent ratings as the best place to retire, the best place to raise a family, and one of the healthiest communities in the United States, etc. Other council members either waffled on the topic or wouldn't take a stand either way, while some accused everyone who is against the MMDs of suffering from reefer madness.

Yet we know that the American Academy of Family Physicians, American Academy of Pediatrics, American College of Emergency Physicians, American Medical Association, American Society of Addiction Medicine, Child Welfare League of America, National Center for School Health Nursing, National Medical Association, and the National Parent Teachers Association took a stand against legalization of marijuana because of the health dangers. Do some council members really think that all of these professionals with doctor degrees and other professionals suffer from reefer madness as well (see chapter 7)? How ludicrous for a community leader to make such a blanket statement.

Dr. Wade Troxel shared a public letter with me that he published.

"Let's be honest about MMDs in Fort Collins.

"On a recent Sunday morning, I watched six young men get off their bikes and march into one of our local pot shops next to CSU campus to become "medicated." Due to the fact that there is no traceability, these "patients" can go from one pot shop to the next on the same day stocking up on their "medicine." We are told Medical Marijuana Dispensaries (MMDs) are "heavily regulated" by the State.

"Let's be honest, MMDs are next to our neighborhoods, child-care providers, schools, commercial districts, and churches increasing from only one in 2007. The City Council voted to grandfather 21 out 23 existing MMDs that failed to meet the separations from residential neighborhoods, child care providers, schools, and churches. The City has ignored its own land-use code and has, in effect, no MMD separations in our community. Where is the compassion for the most impressionable in our community, namely, families with kids, youth and young adults?

"Let's be honest, MMDs have failed Fort Collins and the voters intentions of Amendment 20. If you recall back to its passage in November 2000, Amendment 20 was serve for those with a debilitating medical condition such as "cancer, glaucoma, AIDS, or treatment for such conditions." The

Bluebook of Amendment 20 states clearly that the initiative did not want a MMD retail pot shop model, but a Patient/Caregiver model instead. Well, Fort Collins must be facing glaucoma of epidemic proportions since the rapid increase of MMDs established since 2008.

"Let's be honest, MMDs are not legitimate businesses in the eyes of the Federal government. A July 29, 2011, memo from U.S. Deputy Attorney General James Cole says, "Persons who are in the business of cultivating, selling or distributing marijuana, and those who knowingly facilitate such activities, are in violation of the Controlled Substances Act, regardless of state law." MMDs are entrapping other businesses by perpetuating the myth that they are a business. MMDs cannot obtain loans from banks (due to Federal law) and file income tax returns with IRS by claiming business expenses. Why is the City collecting sales tax on this "medicine"?

"Here are the five things that every voter should know.

1. MMDs are illegal under Federal Law, and they are not recognized as a legitimate business. Marijuana is still a federally controlled substance, Schedule 1 illegal drug.
2. Under Amendment 20, voter intent did not allow for retail distribution on marijuana. MMDs have brought increased crime in Fort Collins with marijuana being noted in law enforcement reports as compared to data before MMDs were established in Fort Collins in 2008.
3. Poudre School District has experienced a significant increase in suspensions and expulsions from marijuana related activity in our schools since MMDs have been established in 2008.
4. Patients will still be able to receive marijuana from a Caregiver, as allowed in Amendment 20, if voters ban marijuana stores on November 1, 2011. There are over 16,000 registered Caregivers in Colorado.
5. More than 75 Colorado communities have already closed MMDs with no reports of lack of access to marijuana from a Caregiver or increases in neighborhood crime.

"Let's be honest and stand up for what's best for our community and not let our town go to pot. Vote "FOR" 300 on November 1st."

CHAPTER 8

Caring for our Youth and Future

Let's Be Honest . . .

We Need to Protect Our Children, Youth, Young Adults, Families, and Elders

The visible presence of an abundance of dispensaries and the advertisement of marijuana as a "medicine" contributes to our youth's growing perception that marijuana is not harmful and is not addictive. It is our responsibility to cultivate an environment that will support the healthy development of our youth . . . who are tomorrow's leaders of our city, the nation, the world.

- Our kids and youth are more important than all the pot shops, marijuana grows, and marijuana candy-making operations.
- Poudre School District attributes a significant increase in middle school and high school students' use of marijuana due to easy access and availability since the MMDs opened.
- Poudre School District reports a 300 percent increase in drug infractions resulting in students' expulsion from school since the arrival of the marijuana dispensaries,
- Today's marijuana is often five to ten times more potent (THC content) than the pot of the '70s. The majority of youth entering drug-abuse treatment report marijuana as their drug of abuse.
- Teens and young adults using marijuana are much more likely to engage in delinquent, dangerous, and violent behaviors.
- Marijuana use has been shown to permanently impair a youth's brain development and negatively affect learning skills, problem solving, concentration, motivation, and memory.

By closing the commercial pot shops, marijuana (MJ) grow operations and MJ candy-making in Ft. Collins, the citizens of Fort Collins will be providing a safer community environment in which to nurture the healthy development of our children, youth, and families.

Protecting Our Kids Is Worth More than Protecting Revenue Streams from Pot Shops

Independent studies have shown that teens who use marijuana are more likely than nonusers to engage in delinquent and dangerous behavior, experience greater depression, three times more likely to have suicidal thoughts, and four times more likely to engage in violent behavior (fights/assaults) (DEA, "DEA Position on Marijuana," July 2010)

Youth using marijuana also have more sexual partners and more likely to engage in unsafe sex. (Bovassco, G., *American Journal of Psychiatry*, 2001)

Marijuana use can permanently impair brain development in youth, particularly in those areas affecting language, memory, and decision making. (Dr. Christian Thurstone, MD, Director, Denver Health—Substance Abuse, Treatment, Education and Prevention Program)

Youth learning skills are negatively affected in terms of concentration, motivation, and memory. Apathy, disrespect, disinterest, dropping out of activities, lower grades, frequent mood changes, depression, isolation from family, etc. are all signs that a teenager is using marijuana. Colorado currently has the third highest rate of marijuana use among youths ages twelve to seventeen. (Dr. Christian Thurstone, MD, Director, Denver Health—Substance Abuse, Treatment, Education and Prevention Program.)

A Fort Collins mom has a daughter who became addicted through her involvement with marijuana, which is "abundantly available" in our city high schools, leading to other drug use. The daughter's care is $5,000 per month (uninsured). Mom says,

"Since this happened to our daughter, I have become aware of many other parents who are in similar situations, but cannot speak out because they are still trying to protect their child's privacy. I speak on their behalf. Not one of them thinks that the dispensaries are making our community safer. They fuel demand."

Marijuana: What's the Truth?

Read what objective experts, scientific research, and well-documented studies have discovered.

TRUTH: Increased use

- The number of teenage and adult users would increase if marijuana was legalized.[2] The number would at least double and most likely triple.
- There are 16.7 million regular marijuana users (6.7 percent of Americans twelve years old or older.)[3] The increase would mean an additional seventeen to thirty-four million users in the United States.
- Colorado could have anywhere from *20 to 30 percent of its teenage population regularly using marijuana.*

Ask yourself: *Do you think increased marijuana use among teenagers and adults is good for Colorado and its future?*

TRUTH: Negative impact on youth

- *Signs that a youth may be using marijuana* are apathy, disrespect, disinterest in activities, lower grades, frequent mood changes, depression, and isolation from the family.
- Teens who use marijuana are more likely than nonusers to engage in delinquent and dangerous behavior.[4]
- Those same teens experience increased risk of schizophrenia and greater levels of depression including being three times more likely to have suicidal thoughts.[4]
- Teens using marijuana are more likely to engage in violent behavior (fights/assaults).[4]
- Marijuana-using teens are more likely to have multiple sexual partners and engage in unsafe sex.[5]

- Marijuana use has been shown to *permanently impair* brain development in youth.[6] Learning skills such as problem solving, concentration, motivation, and memory are negatively affected.
- Of those youth in drug treatment, 68 percent are there for marijuana use.[7] In 2009, eight hundred thirty thousand youth displayed characteristics of marijuana addiction.[8]
- Colorado currently has the nation's third highest rate of marijuana use among youth ages twelve to seventeen.[6]
- Dr. Christian Thurstone says that "in the scientific community, there's no debate about whether or not marijuana is an addictive substance." He says, "We know that marijuana triggers the same parts of the brain as all other addictive substances, like nicotine, cocaine and heroin. Probably about 2 percent of adolescents have an addiction to marijuana, and we know that dependence is not just psychological but physical—and that it includes tolerance levels. Users have to smoke more and more to get the same effect, and there's a withdrawal syndrome that lasts one to two weeks with heavy users." (Dr. Christian Thurstone, a psychiatrist with board certifications in addiction treatment and child and adolescent care, February 1, 20120, Denver Westword Blogs, *http://blogs.westword.com/latestword/2010/02/medical_ marijuana_fallout_heal.php*, accessed March 26, 2012)

Ask yourself: *Would you want your son or daughter to become involved in using marijuana?*

Although Dangers Exist for Marijuana Users of All Ages, Risk is Greatest for the Young.

For them, the impact of marijuana on learning is critical, and pot often proves pivotal in the failure to master vital interpersonal coping skills or make appropriate lifestyle choices. Thus, marijuana can inhibit maturity.

Another concern is marijuana's role as a "gateway drug," which makes subsequent use of more potent and disabling substances more likely. The Center on Addiction and Substance Abuse at Columbia University found adolescents who smoke pot eighty-five times are more likely to use cocaine than their non-pot-smoking peers. And 60 percent of youngsters who use marijuana before they turn fifteen later go on to use cocaine.

But many teens encounter serious trouble well short of the "gateway." Marijuana is, by itself, a high-risk substance for adolescents. More than adults, they are likely to be victims of automobile accidents caused by marijuana's impact on judgment and perception.

Marijuana Dangers

- Impaired perception
- Diminished short-term memory
- Loss of concentration and coordination
- Impaired judgment
- Increased risk of accidents
- Loss of motivation
- Diminished inhibitions
- Increased heart rate
- Anxiety, panic attacks, and paranoia
- Hallucinations
- Damage to the respiratory, reproductive, and immune systems
- Increased risk of cancer
- Psychological dependency

What Students from Different Fort Collins High Schools Are Saying

1. "Medical marijuana dispensaries have made marijuana more accessible and acceptable."
2. "I am disturbed that when I googled 'ice cream stores' and MMDs that there were just as many."
3. "It definitely has affected our conversations in class" (noting that students are talking about how they have access to the MMDs).
4. "Lot of my friends get high during lunch (as a sophomore). "You're the only person that can make the decision."
5. "I look up to the people in the community. The power of influence is by the way you act. I hope I have influenced other students by the way I act."

6. "For a lot of kids, it's not easy to walk away from . . ." (referring to the use of marijuana).
7. "The way to solve this is to find an alternative."
8. "There are those who get it and sell to kids, even when they themselves don't use it. What we have seen is a bright future in the palms of our hands." (Scoot, Director of Team Fort Collins)

The following information was provided by Dr. Jerry Wilson, Poudre School District Superintendent, Fort Collins, Colorado, in response to some public questions about the increased school-expulsion rate since the MMDs opened.

1) This 300 percent drug-related expulsion rate has come out in a lot of arenas with a lot of different tags (marijuana-related, drug-related, etc). Could you clarify that rate for me and what it means? How many students is that?

> "Poudre School District (PSD) has seen the number of drug-related expulsions increase from thirteen in 2008-2009 school year to forty in 2010-2011, which is a 300 percent increase. Students were expelled for either purchasing, selling, or possessing marijuana or another controlled substance. Not every one of the expulsions involved marijuana, but it was a factor in most cases."

2) Do you think that increased rate is a direct effect of the rise of medical marijuana dispensaries? Why or why not?

"While no cause-and-effect relationship is being drawn between the opening of medical *marijuana clinics* in Fort Collins in 2008 and the increased number of drug infractions resulting in expulsion, there appears *to* be an association. Drug related expulsions represented forty of the seventy expulsions in PSD last year. The remaining twenty-nine for "other infractions" has remained relatively steady for the last three years."

3) The drug issue in schools seems to be rising. What's Poudre School District's stance on this (I know that's a pretty straightforward answer), and what's our commitment to fighting that rate?

"Poudre School District has been dealing with drug use by adolescents *for many* years. Last year, the district began implementing alternative to suspension programs in several high schools as a proactive measure to deal with the issue. This program is designed to help keep students in school (because they can't learn if they aren't in class) and also help connect them with resources in the community or through the school to address the underlying causes of the problem. The program looks at educating parents and students about drug use and also helps evaluate situations for individual students, (if you are interested in this program, Tom Lopez, the principal at Rocky Mountain High School is a great resource.)"

4) Anything else I should know? We really want this article to clarify that figure, which has been thrown around in the community quite a bit with Issue 300.

"Poudre School District first publically discussed a concern about the increased discipline for drug infractions in spring 2011 before the political issue was raised. This is not a new issue in schools, but it is one where we are seeing an increasing trend, and we continue to refine our programs and practices to help our students, staff, and parents deal with the ramifications of an uptick in drug use nationwide."

Poudre School District is not the only district in Colorado that noticed a remarkable increase in drug usage where MMDs existed. Hopefully, we all can learn from these trends and start or continue to refine school programs and practices that involve students, teachers, and parents.

Chapter 8 Endnotes

1. *American Council for Drug Eduction's, http://www.acde.org/common/ Marijana.htm*
2. DEA, "Speaking Out Against Drug Legalization," 2003 and 2010 (see document for specific citation)
3. SAMHSA, 2009 Annual Survey on Drug Use and Health, September 2010
4. DEA, "DEA Position on Marijuana," July 2010 (see document for specific citations)
5. Bovassco, G., *American Journal of Psychiatry*, 2001
6. Dr. Christian Thurstone, MD, Director, Denver Health—Substance Abuse, Treatment, Education and Prevention Programs
7. SAMHSA, "Highlights for the 2008 Treatment Episode Data Set"
8. SAMHSA, "2009 National Survey of Drug Use and Health," September 2010
9. The research was prepared by the Healthy and Drug Free Colorado, endorsed by the Colorado Drug Investigators Association.
10. *http://healthydrugfreecolorado.org/default.aspx/MenuItemID/170/ MenuGroup/Home.htm*
11. Dr. Christian Thurstone, M.D., Director, Denver Health—Substance Abuse, Treatment, Education and Prevention Program

CHAPTER 9

The Top Ten Reasons to Not Legalize Marijuana

The top ten reasons not to legalize marijuana was prepared by the Healthy and Drug Free Colorado, endorsed by the Colorado Drug Investigators Association. (1)

10: It Would Still Be Illegal

In July 2011, the federal government reaffirmed marijuana as a Schedule I substance; i.e., no accepted medical use and high abuse potential. Therefore, its possession and use remains a federal crime. Since federal law preempts state law, marijuana would still be illegal in Colorado.

9: Marijuana Possession/Use Is Not Impacting the Criminal Justice System

Proponents often make misleading statements about marijuana arrests and the jail population. In Colorado, the use and possession of less than two ounces (120 to 168 cigarettes) is treated as a traffic violation with a fine and not jail time.

8: Why Repeat Amsterdam's Mistake

The wrong type of people would be attracted to Colorado and for the wrong reasons. We need tourists attracted by our pristine streams and beautiful mountains, not as the Mecca for getting 'stoned.'

7:    Negative Image of Colorado

If marijuana is legalized under Colorado law, our state would be considered the "pot capital" of the nation. This notoriety would have a negative impact on attracting new businesses and families deterred by Colorado's image and quality of life issues. This could also impact decisions to send students to Colorado institutes of higher education.

6:    Harm to Existing Businesses and the Economy

Substance abuse studies have shown that businesses and employers will experience greater rates of absenteeism, industrial accidents, and tardiness as well as less productivity with a potential work force regularly using marijuana. This not only results in economic losses, but conflicts with the federal drug-free-workplace requirements and companies losing federal contracts. Businesses would be less likely to stay or move into a state where drug use related risks are high.

5:    Blindside Economics

At best, potential tax revenue generated by legalizing marijuana will cover only 15 percent of the collateral costs to our community such as: increased drug treatment, emergency-room visits, crime, traffic accidents, and school dropouts, to name just a few of the costs related to marijuana use.

4:    Marijuana Use Would Increase

Marijuana use and its negative health, behavioral, and societal impacts will increase among both youth and adults. The best estimates from experts project that the number of regular users would at least double and likely triple in the most vulnerable twelve-to-twenty-five age range.

3:    Treatment and Addiction Rates Would Rise

Regular marijuana use can be addictive and lead to deteriorating behavior, particularly in young people. In 2009, eight hundred thirty thousand youth had marijuana-addiction characteristics. Sixty-eight percent of youth in drug treatment are there for marijuana use.

2:    Adverse Effect on the Educational Environment

As parents and citizens, we have a responsibility to prepare our youth for a healthy and successful future. The basis for their future lies in providing them with a quality educational environment. If marijuana was legalized, it is estimated that 20 to 30 percent of our school-age children will become regular marijuana users. That will negatively affect their attendance, concentration, memory, brain development and, thus, academic achievement and participation in a positive educational setting.

Walt Disney said, "Our greatest natural resource is the mind of our children." Let's not allow those minds to be polluted with pot.

1:    Deaths from Impaired Driving Would Increase

Marijuana use affects coordination, decision-making, and perception which directly results in impaired driving. Annually, approximately fifty people are killed in Colorado traffic accidents due to people driving under the influence of marijuana. With the increased use of marijuana, we can project that figure will at least double.

These are bold statements, but they can be supported by studies, research, and past experience. For more information, visit *www. healthydrugfreecolorado.org.*

The potential impact of legalizing marijuana is immeasurable. Ask yourself: do we want to make Colorado the country's experimental lab with such potentially devastating human, economic and social costs so a small fraction of people can get stoned with impunity?

It does not pass the common-sense test.

CHAPTER 10

Impaired and Dangerous Driving

Already we are seeing the potential problems if marijuana is legalized in Colorado and the State of Washington, which have ballot measures for their respective states to vote on in 2012. The biggest hurdle is how to measure the volume of marijuana in a person's system to determine if they are fit to drive or not, similar to alcohol? A blood-alcohol test works for alcohol drinkers, but not for marijuana smokers.

Colorado legislatures have battled with the idea of measuring the amount of marijuana in your system through nanograms per milliliter of blood. However, determining actual impairment at the time of driving is problematic. Some states use two nanograms as a guide and others have zero-tolerance laws. Colorado is trying to determine if two or five nanograms is appropriate or not, but their own experts cannot agree.

Dr. Robert DuPont, president of the Institute for Behavior and Health, says that their research shows evidence of "terrible carnage out there on the roads caused by marijuana." Studies related to pot smoking and car accidents indicate that driving after smoking marijuana (drugged driving) may double the risk of being in a critical or deadly crash. In a recent nationwide census of fatal crashes, the percentage of deaths later tested positive for drugs rose 18 percent between 2005 and 2011.

A report about drugged driving by Dr. Robert DuPont, former drug czar for Presidents Ford and Nixon to President Obama's administration, has made this issue a higher priority.

In a PBS Frontline interview of Dr. DuPont, he was quoted as saying: "So when I left the government in 1978, the first thing I did was have a press conference and say, "I was wrong. I made a mistake. Decriminalization is a bad idea. Marijuana is not nonaddictive. In many ways, it's the worst drug of all the illegal drugs. That was a dramatic departure, and I have not wavered since, although many of my friends on that side of the argument are always waiting for me to go back the other way. I switched once, I might switch again. I don't think that's going to happen."

Dr. DuPont's comment that there is evidence of "terrible carnage out there on the roads caused by marijuana," demonstrates another consistent, correlated study from the *Medical Journal of Australia*, February 1977, which denotes cannabis users had twice the usual frequency of traffic accidents in the six to twelve months before they were convicted for cannabis use. Also, cannabis has a much stronger effect than alcohol when it comes to estimation of time and distance. Tests show that while under the influence of cannabis, the breaking action was reduced by 66 percent versus alcohol that was reduced by 44 percent. Here we are, thirty-five years later, with current studies that agree with the previous research years ago.

Driving after smoking even a small amount of marijuana almost doubles the risk of a fatal highway accident, according to an extensive study of 10,748 drivers involved in fatal crashes between 2001 and 2003.

A study by the French National Institute for Transport and Safety Research published in the *British Medical Journal* found that 7 percent of drivers involved in a fatal highway crash used marijuana.

Researchers noted that even small amounts of marijuana could double the chance of a driver suffering an accident and larger doses could more than triple the risk.

Here are some points to think about.

- Marijuana use adversely affects concentration, coordination, and perception, all important skills to safe driving.
- Stanford Medical School research shows that tested pilots were still somewhat impaired on a simulator twenty-four hours after having smoked marijuana.[2]

- In 2009, *28 percent of all fatally injured drivers* tested positive for marijuana use.[3]
- In California, from 2005 to 2010, 1,240 persons were killed in traffic accidents where the driver had used marijuana.[4]
- Last year in Colorado, over fifty people were killed because of marijuana-impaired drivers.[5]
- More people driving on weekend nights were under the influence of marijuana (8.3 percent) than alcohol (2.2 percent).[6]
- A study of 182 truck accidents causing death found 12.8 percent of the drivers were under influence of marijuana and 12.5 percent under the influence of alcohol.[7]
- A study revealed twenty-eight thousand high school seniors admitted to at least one accident after using marijuana.

Ask yourself: do you want more impaired drivers on our interstates and roadways?

Chapter 10 Endnotes

1. SAMHSA, "2009 National Survey of Drug Use and Health," September 2010
2. 13 CNOA, "The Myths of Drug Legalization," 1994
3. Cesar Analysis of 2009 National Highway Transportation and Safety Administration FARS Data
4. Cramer and Associates, "Study Shows Passage of California Cannabis Initiative Will Increase Traffic Deaths"
5. "Drugged Driving Getting Worse in Colorado," 9News.com, 2011 February 17
6. National Highway Traffic Safety Administration Report, 2009
7. Concerned Citizens for Drug Prevention, Inc. citing National Transportation and Safety Board, 1994
8. French National Institute for Transport and Safety Research, published December. 3, 2005, issue of the British Medical Journal, *http://www.bmj.com/content/331/7529/1371.full*, accessed March 22, 2012
9. Read more about Dr. DuPont's interview: *http://www.pbs.org/wgbh/pages/frontline/shows/drugs/interviews/dupont.html#ixzz1pVfL5bXZ*, accessed March 18, 2012
10. *http://seattletimes.nwsource.com/avantgo/2017782727.html*, accessed March 18, 2012

CHAPTER 11

Truth Increased-Risk Employees

- Safety, absenteeism, turnover rate, tardiness, productivity, work quality, and lawsuits are *significant liabilities for employers* with marijuana-using employees.
- Employees who tested positive for marijuana had 55 percent more industrial accidents and 85 percent more injuries compared to those that tested negative on a preemployment exam.[2]
- Employees who abuse drugs are five times more likely than nonusers to injure themselves or coworkers and cause 40 percent of all industrial fatalities.[1]
- Those testing positive for marijuana had absenteeism rates 75 percent higher than those that tested negative.[2]
- A study found that 38 to 50 percent of all workers' compensation claims are related to substance abuse.[3]

Ask yourself: *if you were an employer, would you want to hire an employee who uses marijuana?*

Health insurance companies are unlikely to cover employees with known marijuana medical use. Personal insurance coverage is impossible to secure. In the Web link for InsuranceQuotes.com, their headline story states, "Health Insurance Coverage for Medical Marijuana? No Way, dude!"

Some quotes from the online article states, "Not one major health insurer covers medical marijuana—and there's no indication that it will happen anytime soon. That's because the U.S. Food and Drug Administration has not given its seal of approval to medical marijuana. Why? The federal government still categorizes marijuana as a controlled substance."

"In fact, if a patient acknowledges use of medical marijuana on an application for private health insurance, he'll automatically be declined even though use of the pot is covered by state law," according to Alexandra Eidenberg, president of the Insurance People, an insurance agency in Chicago.

Organizations like the American Cancer Society, American Glaucoma Society, and National Multiple Sclerosis Society have raised health concerns about medical marijuana.

In 2010, Dr. Ed Gogek, a medical marijuana opponent in Arizona, said, "The demand for medical marijuana is not coming from doctors or patient care organizations. It's coming entirely from pot smokers."

Carl Maxey is a business owner of a trucking company and who has worked in the trucking industry for many years, along with his father, Loren Maxey, a former city council member. Mr. Maxey has a unique perspective in how the illegal marijuana industry impacts business owners. I asked Carl to contribute his comments for this book. Carl Maxey wrote,

"When is an illegal business activity good for any community? I cannot think of any, and I believe the community that I grew up in believes that as well. The business community recognizes the many aspects of what it takes to raise a family, educate children, create jobs, manufacture products, and deliver services. The medical marijuana industry discredits many aspects of what the business community has created with honesty and integrity. The growth model for the medical marijuana industry here in Colorado is about getting venerable people from all walks of life a medical marijuana patient card and selling marijuana as "medicine." Prescriptions are given out by doctors, and prescribed medicine is sold through pharmacies. Many employers provide health insurance, and yet this "medicine" and the doctors who prescribe the vast majority are not recognized under any health-benefit plan. The MMD industry has taken an effective caregiver model and created a recreational use demand that has employers very concerned.

"Marijuana is illegal, under the Federal Controlled Substance Act. Many employers have very specific policies that address substance abuse of any type in the work place. Substance abuse leads to increased rates of absenteeism, decreased worker productivity, and increased workplace accidents. For nearly two decades, the Federal Motor Carrier Safety Administration has targeted the use of five Schedule I narcotics and alcohol as a way to reduce accidents and fatalities in the trucking industry. All our nation's commercial drivers are subject to pre-employment, random, and post-accident testing for these substances. Since implementation, accident and fatality rates have been slashed. A study conducted at Stanford Medical School research project in 1992 showed that pilots had significant impairment on a simulator twenty-four hours after having smoked marijuana. Would you ever consider getting on board an airplane where the pilot is self-medicating his "chronic pain"? The facts are very clear; substances of any type in the work place are dangerous to all parties concerned. Business does not have the tools to determine levels of intoxicant with marijuana, so policies will remain as they are. If an employee chooses this type of medication, the consequences will be consistent with company policies. For many employers, this will add to the burden and cost of administration of human resources in their business.

"The rate of growth of young men between the ages of twenty-four and forty obtaining medical marijuana licenses for "chronic pain" is a red flag to employers. In Colorado, Amendment 20 states "Nothing in this section shall require any employer to accommodate the medical use of marijuana in a workplace." This creates a dilemma for employers, insurance companies, and the workman's compensation system. My concern is for the innocent co-worker who may have permanent and/ or life-threatening injuries. The cost and burden to keep our workplaces safe will be borne by increased costs to employers if we continue to normalize this behavior. Ultimately, employers may be forced into using reasonable suspicion or random testing to adequately enforce their policies for the safety of all parties concerned.

"Being part of the business community is more than just employing individuals and collecting taxes. It is about supporting our schools, our nonprofits, the arts, and higher education, and the business community we are a part of. I do not think you will ever see these business owners and their employees going the extra mile, because what they do is illegal under federal law. The medical marijuana store owners cannot bank at your local bank. They cannot donate to the nonprofits, churches, schools, and a variety of other areas within the community. The money is obtained illegally and the transfer of it is money laundering.

"I do not know of any member of our community who wants to deny marijuana to the chronically ill individuals. Medical marijuana dispensers are not needed to accommodate these individuals."

Chapter 11 Endnotes

1. DEA, "Speaking Out Against Drug Legalization," 2003 and 2010 (see document for specific citation)
2. U.S. Department of Health and Human Services, "Marijuana—April 26"
3. National Drug-Free Workplace Alliance, September 21, 2010
4. InsuranceQuotes.com, Health insurance coverage for medical marijuana? No way, dude!, by Brittany Hutson and John Egan, ***http://www.insurancequotes.com/health-insurance-medical-marijuana/***, accessed March 19, 2012

CHAPTER 12

Truth Skyrocketing potency

- Today's marijuana potency is *five times higher* than that of the '70s.
- During the '70s, when marijuana use was at an all-time high, the THC potency was between 1.5 to 3 percent.
- During that same time, users would speak about being stoned, 'wasted, out of it, or spaced out, clearly indicating that even 3 percent potency causes intoxication.
- In 2009, the average THC level was 10 percent which is well over a 300 percent increase from the '70s.[2] Some marijuana has tested at 30% potency.
- At a similar rate for increased potency, there has been a corresponding increase in emergency-room visits for marijuana use.[1]

Ask yourself: *do you think this higher intoxicant level in marijuana is a positive factor for the health and safety of Coloradoans or anywhere?*

In another report from the University of Mississippi's Potency Monitoring Project, they found that the average amount of THC in marijuana, the primary psychoactive ingredient in the drug, was tested at 9.6 percent, which is more than double the potency of marijuana in 1983. The highest concentration of THC found in a single sample was 37.2 percent. This group has researched and collected data on nearly sixty-three thousand marijuana samples since 1975.

According to Dr. Nora Volkow, director of the National Institute on Drug Abuse, "The increases in marijuana potency are of concern since they increase the likelihood of acute toxicity, including mental impairment.

Particularly worrisome is the possibility that the more potent THC might be more effective at triggering the changes in the brain that can lead to addiction; however, more research is needed to establish this link between higher THC potency and higher addiction risk."

While I worked as an undercover drug agent, and throughout the years of my police career, I've steadily watched the potency claims evolve while making various undercover drug transactions; the potency was one of the selling points of the sale.

Chapter 12 Endnotes

1. DEA, "Speaking Out Against Drug Legalization," 2003 and 2010 (see document for specific citation)
2. ONDCP, "New Report Finds Higher Levels of THC in U.S. Marijuana to Date," May 2009
3. *Los Angeles Times* | Health, Marijuana more potent than ever, June 12, 2008, by Janet Cromley, *http://latimesblogs.latimes.com/booster_ shots/2008/06/marijuana-more.html*, accessed March 22, 2012

Half the load of 1 ton of marijuana purchased near Nogales, AZ, destined for Northern Colorado communities in 1973. Marijuana is packed in kilo bricks.

CHAPTER 13

Truth Additional adverse Effects

- Despite assertions to the contrary, *marijuana is addictive*. More than four million Americans are classified as meeting the criteria for marijuana addiction.[17]
- Of emergency-room visits, 374,000 people were there because of a primary marijuana problem.[18]
- Marijuana smoke contains 50 percent to 70 percent more cancer-causing agents than smoked tobacco.[19]
- Only 0.7 percent of all state inmates are there for marijuana possession, with many pleading down from more serious crimes.[20] In Colorado, possession of less than two ounces of marijuana (between 120 to 168 marijuana cigarettes) although illegal, is only a citable offense with a $100 fine.
- Taxing marijuana to create revenue is "blind side economics." Based on the experience with heavily taxed alcohol and cigarettes, revenue from marijuana would cover less than 15 percent of the societal cost associated with the adverse consequences of increased marijuana use.

Ask yourself: *do you think it enhances Colorado's future or attracts quality people and businesses to be considered the Pot Capital of the U.S.?*

If you answered no to any one of the previous questions, then you should also say no to legalize marijuana for recreational use.

Bill Clinton's head of drug policy said, "U.S. law does not grant people the right to destroy themselves or others . . ." He endorsed the continuing prohibition on drugs because "studies show that the more a product is available and legitimized, the greater will be its use . . . if drugs were legalized, the cost to the individual and society would grow astronomically."(21)

Let's not forget that researchers have also found that marijuana fungus can cause infections. Research at the Medical College of Wisconsin in Milwaukee revealed that half the marijuana users studied were infected by fungi belonging to the aspergillus family. Dr Steven Kagen, along with other researchers, noted that people who smoke marijuana inhale large amounts of fungal spores of many types. "We have yet to find a sample of marijuana that doesn't have fungal organisms in it." His research appears in a letter to the *New England Journal of Medicine*, February 19, 1981. "Growing organisms can cause a number of lung diseases that range from asthma to fatal infections."

With the prolific growth of marijuana in homes, basements, garages, etc., such sites are more than likely going to have fungus. When I worked in drug enforcement, we found many grow operations with hydro pod systems and other grows in sheds and basements.

Fort Collins Police Detectives search a basement with a growing/drying operation in Fort Collins, CO (late 1980's)

—photographed by Ray Martinez

We also are learning that when comparing marijuana smoking to cigarettes, the impact is horrendous; one joint of marijuana is equivalent to smoking twenty cigarettes. According to a group of scientists in New Zealand, in the high-exposure group, lung cancer risk rose by 5.7 times for patients who smoked more than a joint a day for ten years, or two joints a day for five years, after adjusting for other variables, including cigarette smoking.

"Cannabis smokers end up with five times more carbon monoxide in their bloodstream (than tobacco smokers)," team leader Richard Beasley, at the Medical Research Institute of New Zealand, said in a news release, January 29, 2008.

The irony of this New Zealand study by Richard Beasley is that a very similar report was made by UCLA in 1978. In a UCLA study, researcher found that smoking five joints had the same effect on human lungs as smoking 112 cigarettes. This is due, in part, to the fact that marijuana has more cancer-causing compounds than does an equal amount of tobacco. Here we are, thirty years later and the studies are consistently proving the detrimental dangers of marijuana.

In another study report done in 1976, Dr. J. Hall of Kingston Hospital, Jamaica, reports that an emphysema-bronchitis syndrome is a well-recognized finding among black male laborers using marijuana.

Drs. H. Kolansky and W. Moore, two Philadelphia psychiatrists wrote in a classic paper in 1971: "These patients consistently showed very poor social judgment, poor attention span, poor concentration, confusion, anxiety, depression, apathy, passivity, indifference, and often, slowed and slurred speech . . ." This too is consistent with current studies. How much proof do we need before we can come around from the wall of denial and admit the danger to our youth?

I often keep notes on information that I have received over the years. Finding one particular set of notes, I was refreshed with the memory of watching a television special aired December 10, 1978, when kids were interviewed about their marijuana-smoking addiction. Some of the students admitted openly to smoking twenty, thirty, even fifty marijuana joints a week. One fifteen-year-old estimated he smoked about one hundred reefers weekly!

Yet we hear people argue that marijuana is not addictive. Come on, let's face reality. Let's be honest, the science admits it and so do the youth. Why do some adults find it difficult to come to grips with authenticity? I'm starting to understand why.

According to Dr. Christian Thurstone, a psychiatrist with board certifications in addiction treatment and child-and-adolescent care, "Good research shows that using marijuana makes anxiety, depression, and ADHD worse, so let's stop prescribing marijuana to our youth . . . About 95 percent of the hundreds of young people referred to my clinic each year have problems with marijuana . . . I recently reviewed medical marijuana licenses in Colorado and found that only 3 percent belong to people with cancer and 1 percent to people with HIV. Those illnesses are not open to much interpretation; you've either got them or you don't. However, a whopping 90 percent of Colorado's medical marijuana licenses have been awarded for 'pain,' which is a highly subjective qualifying condition that makes it easy to abuse the system . . . Also stunning is that marijuana has bypassed the Colorado Prescription Drug Monitoring Program, which enables me to look up all of my patients' prescriptions. Now, I can see all of their meds—except for their marijuana."

Dr. Christian Thurstone is a board-certified child/adolescent and addictions psychiatrist who conducts federally funded research on marijuana addiction in teenagers.

The great news is that most of our youth do not use marijuana; that in itself is refreshing.

Chapter 13 Endnotes

1. DEA, "Speaking Out against Drug Legalization," 2003 and 2010 (see document for specific citation)
2. SAMHSA, 2009 Annual Survey on Drug Use and Health, September 2010
3. DEA, "DEA Position on Marijuana," July 2010 (see document for specific citations)
4. Bovassco, G., *American Journal of Psychiatry*, 2001
5. Dr. Christian Thurstone, MD, Director, Denver Health—Substance Abuse, Treatment, Education and Prevention Programs
6. SAMHSA, "Highlights for the 2008 Treatment Episode Data Set"
7. SAMHSA, "2009 National Survey of Drug Use and Health," September 2010
8. 13 CNOA, "The Myths of Drug Legalization," 1994
9. Cesar Analysis of 2009 National Highway Transportation and Safety Administration FARS Data
10. Cramer and Associates, "Study Shows Passage of California Cannabis Initiative Will Increase Traffic Deaths"
11. "Drugged Driving Getting Worse in Colorado," 9News.com, 2011 February 17
12. National Highway Traffic Safety Administration Report, 2009
13. Concerned Citizens for Drug Prevention, Inc. citing National Transportation and Safety Board, 1994
14. U.S. Department of Health and Human Services, "Marijuana—April 26"
15. National Drug-Free Workplace Alliance, September 21, 2010
16. ONDCP, "New Report Finds Higher Levels of THC in U.S. Marijuana to Date," May 2009
17. National Institute of Drug Abuse, "Marijuana," 2010
18. ONDCP, Director Kerlikowske Speech, March 4, 2010
19. ONDCP, "Marijuana: Know the Facts," October 2010
20. Bureau of Justice Assistance Report, "Substance Abuse and Treatment, State and Federal Prisoners," January 1999

21. *Washington File*, U.S. Department of State, 14 March 2000 see *http:// usinformation.state.gov/topical/global/drugs/monsen.htm* as at 10 April 2002, quote of President Bill Clinton's head of drug policy

22. FoxNews.com, Smoking one joint is equivalent to 20 cigarettes, Study Says, published January 29, 2008, *http://www.foxnews.com/ story/0,2933,326309,00.html#ixzz1pX46G2m4*, accessed March 18, 2012

23. UCLA study comparing the impact of tobacco cigarettes to marijuana consumption, Coloradoan, by Bruce Blackwell, Gannett News Service, New York, December 7, 1978

24. Journal of the AAPN, Vol. 1, No. 1, 1976, "Chronic Effects of Cannabis"

25. Denver Post, Posted: 01/31/2010 01:00:00 AM MST, Updated: 02/01/2010 02:11:14 PM MST, Opinion Letter by Dr. Thurstone, *Smoke and mirrors: Colorado teenagers and marijuana—Denver Post http://www.denverpost. com/opinion/ci_14289807#ixzz1qFFpZmTm*, accessed March 26, 2012

CHAPTER 14

Colorado Organizations Opposed
to Legalization of Marijuana

Clearly, many professional organizations, including health agencies, do not support the legalization of marijuana. This isn't a case of reefer madness as the opponents would like you to believe. These are educated people who are concerned about the future of Colorado youth.

- American Academy of Pediatrics, Colorado Chapter
- The Center for Family Care
- Boys and Girls Clubs of Metro Denver
- Colorado Alliance for Drug Endangered Children
- Colorado Mothers, Inc.
- Early Childhood Council of Logan, Phillips and Sedgwick Counties
- Educating Voices, Inc.
- Girl Scouts of Colorado
- National Association of Counsel for Children
- Partners Mentoring Youth
- Prevent Child Abuse Colorado
- Society for Adolescent Health and Medicine, Rocky Mountain Chapter
- Students Taking Action Not Drugs (STAND.)
- Teen Challenge of the Rocky Mountains
- Urban Peak Colorado Springs Shelter for Homeless and Runaway Youth
- Coaches of Excellence Institute, Inc.
- Roaring Fork School District Board of Education
- Focus on the Family
- International Faith Based Coalition

- New Life Church, Colorado Springs
- Chabot Strategies, LLC
- Coffee for Conservatives
- Colorado State Fire Chiefs' Association
- Freestyle Foundation, Inc.
- Historic Rail Adventures, LLC (Georgetown, CO)
- IDEA of Denver, Inc.
- Stars and Stripes United, Inc.
- Benevolent and Protective Order of Elks—Colorado Drug Awareness Program
- Benevolent and Protective Order of Elks—National Drug Awareness Program
- Colorado Elks Lodge Association
- A Turning Point Colorado
- Advocates for Recovery
- Alice's Place—an Empowerment Center
- The Courage to Change Addiction Recovery Ranch
- Treatment Providers Alliance of Colorado
- Citizens Against Legalizing Marijuana (CALM)
- Drug Free America Foundation
- The Drug Free Projects Coalition
- Drug-Free Kids: America's Challenge
- The Drug-Free Schools Coalition
- East High School PTSA Substance Abuse and Prevention Committee
- El Paso and Teller Counties Alliance for Drug Endangered Children
- Institute on Global Drug Policy
- International Scientific and Medical Forum on Drug Abuse
- Meth Free Delta County
- National Drug Free Workplace Alliance
- Nip It in the Bud USA
- PRIDE—Omaha, Inc
- The Rural Law Enforcement Methamphetamine Initiative
- Save Our Society from Drugs (SOS.)
- Safe and Healthy Mesa County
- Take Back America Campaign
- TEAM Fort Collins
- Westminster Area Community Awareness Action Team

- Association of Colorado State Patrol Professionals
- The Aurora Police Association
- Colorado Association of Chiefs of Police
- Colorado Association of School Resource Officers (CASRO)
- Colorado Drug Investigators Association
- Colorado Law Enforcement Officers Association
- Colorado State Fire Chiefs' Association
- Colorado State Patrol Professionals
- Colorado State Lodge Fraternal Order of Police
- County Sheriff's of Colorado
- Denver Police Protective Association
- The National Latino Peace Officers Association—Colorado State Chapter
- Retired Peace Officers of Colorado
- Rocky Mountain Chapter of the Society of Former Special Agents of the FBI
- Colorado Attorney General John Suthers
- Christy McCampbell, former Deputy Assistant Secretary for the U.S. Department of State, International Narcotics and Law Enforcement Affairs
- Ronald C. Sloan, Director, Colorado Bureau of Investigation
- Colonel James M. Wolfinbarger, Chief, Colorado State Patrol

Chapter 14 Endnotes

1. Proclamation for Colorado's public health and safety, we are opposed to legalizing marijuana for recreational use: *http://healthydrugfreecolorado. org/default.aspx/MenuItemID/181/MenuSubID/31/MenuGroup/Home.htm*

CHAPTER 15

Signs of Marijuana Use (and Marijuana Deaths)

There are many signs of marijuana use to be aware of. We have listed numerous below to help in determining if someone you care for may be using marijuana.

Physical Characteristics:	Behavioral Characteristics
• Bloodshot/glassy eyes • Enlarged (dilated) eye pupils • Impaired short term memory • Red, puffiness under the eyes • Sleepiness /Sleepy appearance • Discolored fingers • Difficulty thinking • Distorted sensory perceptions • Dry mouth • Euphoria (temporary feelings of elation, energy, and limitless power) • Feeling sluggish • Impaired judgment • Impaired short-term memory • Increased heart rate • Increased appetite, craving sweets • Reduced coordination	• Increased appetite • Craving for sweets • Reduced motivation • Anxiety • Grandiosity (acting in a pompous or boastful manner) • Inappropriate laughter; giggle and act silly (for no reason) **Drug Paraphernalia** • Cigarette-rolling papers • Seeds that have been cleaned from marijuana • Smell on clothing, in room, or in vehicle • Pipes, bongs, homemade smoking devices (you may see sticky residue from burned marijuana)

• Temporary feelings of reduced anxiety or stress • Sadness/depressed mood • Sensation that time is passing slowly • Burnt fingertips • Eating binges • Droopy eyes	• Social withdrawal and isolation • Small seeds in the lining of pockets • Strong odor of burnt leaves • Use of incense • Incense, breath mints to hide odor **Withdrawal Symptoms:** • Irritability • Agitation • Insomnia • Difficulty remembering/ learning • Depression

Warning Signs that Marijuana Use is a Problem

- Altered perception of reality (e.g., hallucinations, delusions, and suspicious thoughts).
- Continued marijuana use despite significant problems related to use (e.g., financial/legal problems or neglecting responsibilities)
- Craving marijuana
- Finding it increasingly difficult to resist using marijuana when it is available
- Spending a great deal of time in activities necessary to obtain marijuana
- Cutting back or stopping important social, occupational, or recreational activities because of marijuana use
- Unsuccessful attempts to control or cut down use

Signs and Symptoms of Cannabis-Related Overdose and Deaths

Excessive use of marijuana can create paranoia and possible psychosis. These same effects may develop from long-term use of the drug, which has also been observed to produce sharp personality changes, especially in adolescent users.

- lung damage
- chronic bronchitis
- lowering of testosterone
- acute anxiety attacks
- chronic reduction of attention span
- possible birth defects, stillbirths, and infant deaths

1. Marijuana is usually smoked using cigarette rolling papers, a purchased water bong, or a makeshift bong that can be made from a variety of items.
2. Hash can be smoked or eaten and is sometimes cooked into baked goods.

Generally it can be difficult to recognize marijuana use if you don't see the individual after smoking when they are still experiencing the effects of the drug. The potency of marijuana has increased exponentially in the past twenty years.

Deaths

There is a constant sounding of the bell that marijuana doesn't induce deaths. We used to not have reported deaths caused by people smoking cigarettes. However, as time and researched advanced, we have learned that tobacco smoking is responsible for over four hundred thousand deaths a year.

We should clear the air and understand that there may not be any *reported causes of death* due to smoking marijuana. Hold on though, the Australian Bureau of Statistics (ABS) documents 184 cannabis-related deaths during 1997-2001. Marijuana (cannabis) is often one factor in a ply-drug cocktail that causes death, including alcohol as one of the combinations of use.

The Drug Abuse Warning Network in the United States, reports that those counties in which medical examiners tested for cannabis, of the 664 reported cannabis-related deaths in 1999, 28 percent (187) involved cannabis only.

According to Britain's most senior coroner, marijuana use is a lot more dangerous than believed and hundreds of young people die each year in "accidents" caused by their prolonged use of the drug.

Hamish Turner, the president of the Coroners' Society, told the *Telegraph* that the marijuana has increasingly been the cause of deaths that were reported as accidents or suicides.

Mr. Turner stated that "Cannabis is as dangerous as any other drug and people must understand that it kills. From my long experience I can say that it is a very dangerous substance. Increasingly it is mentioned not only as the first drug taken by people who overdose, but also in suicides and accidental deaths.

"Many go on to harder drugs and I am dealing with more and more heroin overdoses. People can also suffer severe consequences from the cannabis alone, however."

Consider what the White House Office of National Drug Control Policy reports.

The Drug Abuse Warning Network (DAWN) collects information on deaths involving drug abuse that were identified and submitted by 128 death investigation jurisdictions in 42 metropolitan areas across the United States. Cannabis ranked among the 10 most common drugs in 16 cities, including Detroit (74 deaths), Dallas (65), and Kansas City (63). Marijuana is very often reported in combination with other substances; in metropolitan areas that reported any marijuana in drug abuse deaths, an average of 79 percent of those deaths involved marijuana and at least one other substance.[4]

Chapter 15 Endnotes

1. *Marijuana Addition Information and Treatment http://www. marijuanaaddiction.information/marijuana-signs-of-use.htm*
2. From News Weekly, March 8 2003, By Richard Egan, Marijuana may be causing deaths, *http://www.katinkahesselink.net/health/canabis.html*, accessed March 22, 2012
3. The Telegraph, "Cannabis use causes 'hundreds of deaths a year', coroner warns" February 2003, *http://alcoholism.about.com/b/a/039646.htm*, and *http://www.allaboutworldview.org/human-suffering.htm*, accessed March 22, 2012
4. Substance Abuse and Mental Health Services Administration, Mortality Data from the Drug Abuse Warning Network, 2001 (PDF), January 2003, see http://dawninformation.samhsa.gov/old_dawn/pubs_94_02/mepubs/ files/ DAWN2001/DAWN2001.pdf.

CHAPTER 16

The E-mail References:
American Weed, National Geographic TV Show

Since the show *American Weed* was aired on the National Geographic channel, starting in February 2012, I received numerous e-mails. The portrayal of the show illustrated a biased leaning toward the marijuana dispensaries that were selling marijuana illegally. National Geographic producers consistently showed the opposition's viewpoint for an average of ten minutes, to our viewpoint of approximately two minutes. They took clips of conversations of mine and others that were enough to "stir the pot" instead of giving a balanced report. The program consisted of eleven episodes, one hour each. Throughout the programs, the opposition was allowed to comment on our statements, but we were never given the opportunity to comment on the opposition's statements.

The TV episodes mimicked a reality show with the opposition, particularly with one family of brothers. Throughout the shows, they were depicted as a poor family that was being picked on, and their business was being ruined by us; one of the brothers referred to me as "an evil man." Each show contained a segment of them either having a snowball fight, playing hide-and-go-seek, joshing with each other by trapping one of the brothers under a cellar door, sitting around on a porch playing a guitar and singing, pulling hair off their chest, and them showing their mother and grandmother a marijuana flower sitting in a family circle; you would think they were part of *The Waltons* weekly TV program. However, our side of the show did not touch on any personal family gatherings or lifestyle of anyone other than a small clip of the orphanage building I was raised in until age five.

Naturally, with that kind of television choreography, I would receive negative e-mails from people who were irate with the limited broadcast given to those of us who were spelling out the truth. Most of the comments received contain a lot of vulgar language and personal insults, which add to the validity of what substance abuse and addiction can do to the voice of reason. Occasionally, I received some good comments. The following are e-mails as I received them. However, I couldn't print all of them, but you will get the jest of the behavior of most of my e-mails.

Please read with caution, knowing the extreme vulgar language used by the writers, whom in most cases are anonymous and have phony e-mails. I have deliberately changed some of the vulgar words into "?!!?!?" so children and others don't have to read the actual words. Most of the e-mails I received contain fake e-mail addresses, and those e-mail addresses contained insulting e-mail names (deliberately designed that way to add insult through their irrational behavior). Someone once said that a person's true character is revealed behind a mask. There is a lot of masks covering these e-mails and the couple of hundred e-mails that I received that are not in this publication.

I do not hold any animosity toward any of these people, knowing there is a deep-seated problem beyond my ability to help. Nevertheless, I chose to incorporate the e-mails to illustrate illogical behavior that may have been triggered by marijuana abuse:

Name: Jake Kienholz
E-mail: jakekienholz@gmail.com

Message: Watching you spew misinformation about medical marijuana is repulsive. Have you ever spoken with Medical Marijuana patients or do you just get your misinformation from government propaganda. If you ever had a single shred of intelligence in your brain you would do research before you attack medical marijuana patients. LOOK AT ACTUAL CASE STUDIES you moron . . . SPEAK to SEVERAL patients!! Its not just for hippies. There is too much information out there to deny the benefits of marijuana. Denying this would be the equivalent of denying that the holocaust happened. You're not one of those people are you? The ignorance is parallel.

Here's a starting point to end your ignorance:

http://www.cannabis-med.org/studies/study.php

EDUCATED YOURSELF, stop being so ignorant.

An Oregon MM patient

(After sending Jake a response with some specific research and data, here is how he responded.)

So which pharmaceutical company lines your pockets? I will respond within the next few days to debunk MOST of this unfounded BS . . . Don't send me "government" studies or studies from biased Religious fanatic doctors, but actual independent studies. You're a complete idiot if you swallow every so-called "fact" the government presents to you. I've spoken with Harvard educated MD's, I've seen the research myself, I know from personal experience and in speaking with hundreds of MM patients. Do you honestly believe everything you are told? ANSWER THIS QUESTION: Have you PERSONALLY met with and spoken with Medical Marijuana patients and truly listened to them? Do you have any idea of the damage done to the body from prescription drugs? Do you understand that normal everyday people turn to medical marijuana simply because of the side effects of prescription drugs? Can you sit there and tell me that alcohol is a better recreational drug? Here's some facts from the *CDC*. I laugh at your section on deaths from marijuana when I'm sure you have been impaired driving home after a few drinks. Don't lie to yourself Ray. Speaking from personal experience, alcohol is by far worse for your body and even worse on society. Don't be a *hypocrite*. How about some information on prescription *overdosing:*) Have fun with that too. It is physically impossible to overdose from Marijuana.

Do you know what the term "propaganda" means? Well before our government ever studied the effects of marijuana they were telling people that you become a crazed rapist murderer if you smoke it. Case in point the movie Refer Madness (which is now in the Comedy section). It will take time to un-condition people like you and your brainwashed ignorance. In fact I bet you have a large portion of investments in Pharmaceuticals dont you . . . The government finally apologized for slavery in 2008, one day they will apologize to the millions of people incarcerated for non-violent marijuana offenses. Have you ever smoked marijuana in your life???

In case you are wondering, I have a condition called Cyclic Vomiting Syndrome. I have a prescription for *Dilaudid* (read about it) which I do not take because it makes my condition 10x worse. I eat edibles which is the safest way to consume so don't feed me BS about it being unhealthy. BTW—The dioxides a person consumes from smoking (not vaporizing) are fewer than sitting around a common camp fire. Did you know THC reduces lung cancer cells from growing? *Read.* in fact more studies have come out to support this as well. You sir are the uneducated person as it related to this topic. I would LOVE to wax intellectual on this topic for hours on end with you but your ignorance is your bliss. So if you don't feel like getting an education from a 32 year old, then you should do it yourself. You are fighting an illogical fight with illogical rationale. There will always be a criminal element just as kids can buy Vicodin, Oxy's and other pills illegally just as easy as pot. Legalize it, you can better control and regulate it. **I am all in favor of revoking someone's MM license if they use it illegally.** Whether it's legal or not, people will still seek it out. I'd rather buy it from a dispensary that tests for mold spores, spider mites, and other potentially dangerous pesticides, etc. than buying it from an underground black market where quality/health is not a concern. Does that make sense? If it doesn't than I just feel sorry for you Ray.

Sincerely,
An over-educated Oregonian

P.S. The FDA is ok with feeding this country processed garbage, hence the size of the health epidemic we have in this country. I would not trust the FDA to administer Medical Marijuana but agree it needs to be regulated and administered by an independent agency WITH government oversight.

The only question I have is the position of one of your drug pushing detractors concerning the Holocaust. Don't drug pushers believe that the Holocaust occurred?

Again, thank you for your courageous efforts in stemming the tide of illegal drugs like marijuana.

Anonymous
Sent from my "I" Phone

Name: CHRIS ROGERS
E-mail: BLANDON864@YAHOO.COM

Message: YA KNOW, I DON'T HAVE A QUESTION BUT I DO WANNA SAY WHY ARE YOU TRYING TO STOP THE MEDICAL POT DISPENSIERY'S? THAT'S B!??!?!? AND THERE IS A REASON AS TO WHY YOUR BITCH ASS DID NOT STAY MAYOR LONGER THAN YOU DID! WHAT IF THAT WAS YOU THAT HAD THOSE PROBLEMS THE PATIENTS HAD, YOU WOULD BE THINKING DIFFERENT I BET THAT! YOU NEED TO GO F!?! YOURSELF AND STOP WITH THE B!??!?!? YOUR TRYING TO PULL! THERE IS A TAX ON POT EVER SINCE THE 1800'S! I WATCH WEEDS AND THE MORE I WATCH IT, THE MORE I SEE HOW MUCH OF A D!?! YOU REALLY ARE! JUST BE GLAD I DON'T LIVE OUT THERE CAUSE IF I SAW YOU ON THE CURB WITH THOSE B!??!?!? VOTE 300 SIGNS, I WOULD DEFINITELY MAKE A SEEN INFRONT OF THE WHOLE COUNTY! GROW THE F!?! UP AND LET IT BE ESPECIALLY SINCE THERE ARE SO MANY MEDICAL BENEFICIARIES TO MARAJUANA!

Name: Tom Jones
E-mail: thisforfree@gmail.com

Message: Why don't you do something productive with your life? Why you don't you try to get something that actually harms people made illegal? Like prescription pain pills? Instead, you would rather have people addicted to pain pills instead of smoking marijuana, which does no damage or has ever killed anyone. Please show me where there has been a death from a overdose of marijuana. It is a PLANT that grows out of the ground. Are you going against something that GOD himself put on this earth? I hope one day someone in your family has a condition to where they could have been treated with marijuana and would have had no side effects, but instead, they will get a nice bottle of percocet or oxycontin, which they will slowly become addicted to and lose their quality of life. Do you realize you cannot become addicted to marijuana? If you smoke everyday for a week and then stop you will be fine. You are wasting your life and your time. Do something better with yourself, stop trying to ruin peoples lifes. Some people really do need the medicine they are taking, and by medicine I mean marijuana.

Name: steve
E-mail: *nucklehead71@hotmail.com*

Message: I'm sure that you have had some pretty enlightening e-mails concerning your campaign against medical marijuana, but let me tell you something Mr. Martinez, I think that you are one of those poor orphans who has developed a severe inferiority complex due to your own parents giving you away and not loving you the way they should have. Just because you have had some hardships, and a position in local government, doesn't give you the right to take away a perfectly natural medicine from the people who need it. I also think that you don't even have your facts straight about it to begin with. I think that you are a close minded idiot who just wants some kind of recognition to make yourself feel better (EGO)! I personally would like to say that it is my opinion that you sir should reevaluate your stance on this issue for the sake of all those in pain! I really don't know how you can sleep at night knowing that you have just increased the black market crime in you township to a height that will be higher than what it has ever been. In closing, I think you are a spineless, week minded, and selfish person who is really breathing the air that the rest of us good Americans should be breathing. Do us all a huge favor and just shut the f!?! up! You're a misinformed errand boy for the fascist's out there that want to take away all of our GOD given rights as well as our civil liberties! I hope you rot in hell for what you have done to all of those innocent people out there! You SUCK!!!!!!!!!!!!!!!!!!!!!!!!!

yours,
nucklehead71

ps—go jump off a cliff or something at least then the buzzards can make some use of you worthless carcass.

Name: Troy
E-mail: gorgedishtech@yahoo.com

Message: Did you do your homework before prop 300? Do it now. How many jobs have you eliminated? How many people are now having to break the law to get meds that they were getting legally? Are you a medical doctor, or just reading one-sided literature reguarding the topic and felt bored one day? How much in tax revenue is your community losing now? How many fewer school books does that add up to? How many Department of Health programs are going to be cut because of the lose of tax money? You have single handedly destroyed the community you say you are trying to help and protect. Please do your homework and know if you ever came to the northwest, we will destroy you before you have the chance to ruin our quailty of life and our right as American citizens to choose.

Name: Anonymous
E-mail: damnkid808@yahoo.com

Message: Hello Mr. Martinez, allow me to introduce myself as anonymous. I am here to talk to you about the medical marijuana situation in fort collins, in which if the bill to ban these dispensaries were to go through hundreds of patients would go without proper medication. some of said patients have severe pains and aches and are unable to function without the use of medical marijuana. I ask you the person himself how you would feel if you had severe pains and aches and your medicine that worked so well at keeping said pain at bay were to just be taken from you. What I'm trying to tell you Mr. Martinez is to quit being such an ignorant ass and actually research marijuana instead of automatically shooting it down. You will find that it is much more than how you think of it as a "black market drug" or a hazardous substance, in all honesty it is a plant that is grown from the earth just as any other plant is. There are also healthy ways of using marijuana. For example vaporizing extracts the most amount of THC with little to none of the effects of traditional smoking. I also want to state that I do not advocate the ABUSE of marijuana, I personally use it as a recreational mental stimulant. As for your claims that dispensaries have "no knowledge of the amount of THC their strains contain" that is a false accusation, for dispensaries know exactly how much THC their strains contain and exactly what type of high each strain gives off. and even if they did not it is impossible to over dose on marijuana, unlike methamphetamine, or cocaine or even alcohol for that matter. the effect from an overdose of marijuana is a good nights sleep. In closing I hope this message does not carry an implication of "I'm right and you're wrong" because I believe neither side is either of those. I am merely suggesting that you come to a compromise with smokers instead of automatically assuming them as bad people, because majority of them are not. Marijuana makes people happy and the sad truth is that no one will ever know pure happiness until they at least try it. So I encourage you Mr Martinez to take a little toke and truly feel alright for once.

From: Titus Andronicus

I saw on National Geographic and you come across as a truly a sad and confused individual. You are grossly misinformed about the facts relating to medical marijuana use, patients, and crime statistics.

You come off as a close minded, ignorant old man with no real purpose in life so you have to find something do with your time to keep busy so you have decided to crusade against something you clearly do not understand or have a real grasp of. When I want to define what misinformed propaganda is to someone I point them towards you as a perfect example of that.

I am NOT a marijuana user myself but I am an American and I believe personal freedoms. I am a father of two amazing children and you are the face I show them when I teach them about closed mindedness, ignorance and what it looks like when someone is more concerned with imposing their personal opinions on others with no regard for their personal beliefs or decisions. You are the epitome of un-American.

This country was founded on the principles of freedom and liberty.

Since you cannot be trusted with personal responsibility you want the government to strip away those freedoms from others. Just because your birth parents weren't responsible enough to raise you and love you like good parents should doesn't mean you should hold a grudge on society and want everyone else freedoms stripped away.

You need to spend some time with an open mind and get educated on the real facts. Not just looking for propaganda and incorrect information that suits your biased agenda. You also come across as a deeply insecure and unhappy person which I do pity you for and hope for you to overcome that day. I strongly suggest you seek out some personal therapy as it appears on the surface you have some deeper issues you are trying suppress.

Name: James
E-mail: killthestate@hotmail.com

Message: Ray Martinez is the most stupid idiot I have ever seen on tv. He continues to prove his stupidity by being on the air. I suggest he goes and gets an education.

Ray Martinez your a c!?! whore

Name: rob
E-mail: beavis.butthead99@hotmail.com

Message: your scum on earth, let the weed be free

Name: Jacob
E-mail: Kooooter66@hotmail.com

Message: Question How many buisness currently sell alchol or cigs. You are just a fear monger out to control anything they let you. you are everthing that is wrong with this country. stop trying to control me I dont tell you how to run your life and its clear you have no knowledge of the benifits of cannabis.

Name: Tammy
E-mail: kevtam07@sbcglobal.net

Message: Mr Martinez, I respectively write to you in hopes to help you understand what chronic pain does to ones life. I have dealt with chronic pain since I was 10 yrs old. I have degenerative disk disease. My doctors have had me on every pain pill you can think of through the years. I worry so much what this is doing to my liver, kidneys etc. I face so much depression because of the pain and even though I take very strong meds I'm still robbed of a decent life. My neck is completely fused together and my back is also partially fused If I could use medical marijuana and if it would give me a better quality life how can you or anyone take that away from me? People that dont experience the pain that I and others do can in no way know what we go through. I would bet there are more abuses made with prescription medication than ever with medical marijuana. If it was legal where i live then I would use it. I HATE MY PAIN PILLS! There are days that I cry before having to take them in the morning. I'm just asking that you be careful before judging people that use medical marijuana for pain.

Name: Puddy Tat
E-mail: darkangl27@hotmail.com

Message: Ray I sent you a request for all these facts and you have not responded.

Stat's req:

40% crime increase—sense medical MJ has come into affect.

97% of people are just going in and claiming back pain to get a card—While only 6% have enough pain in your eyes to be able to gain access to ALT medications—where do these numbers come from?

You made a blanket statment that all these Medical MJ places don't know the THC content nor the difference between the strains of medication—have you asked them yourself?

Ray I expect answers from you directly please respond!

Name: For a free America
E-mail: Raythecommunist@communist.com

Message: Why are you such a terrible person? Why do you think it is ok to make decisions for other people? Marijuana helps people in pain. My hope is that you get sick with cancer and need to feel better and the very drug you pushed to ban will not be there for you . . . and you suffer everyday. Liberty and justice for all . . . means I should have the choice to make my own decision for myself not you.

People like you make me sick and disappointed to be an American.

Name: kyle
E-mail: kxxxxalize215@aol.com
Message: Mr. Ray Martinez,

My name is Kyle, i am from Highlands Ranch, CO. i am watching you on American Weed and all I have to say is go pick up a book about marijuana. I am 16 years old and is more information about this topic than you. you have your facts wrong. I smoke marijuana every day and maintain a 3.7 GPA, I also keep up my job. You believe that the medical marijuana dispensary make marijuana more available to our kids and teens. take this from a teenager, marijuana is more accessible than alcohol or tobacco for me. if you have done your homework you would know marijuana is virtually non-lethal. Think about it, if you want to get rid of the medical marijuana, your

not decreasing the demand. by making it illegal you only put the
money in the hands of criminals and cartels, besides putting in the
hands of the government where they could spend it on something
smart like education. if your reading this and think i am just some
lazy pot head then your just stubborn. all i ask is to learn the other
side of the story your thinking is very bias. go pick up a book and
get your facts right.

from,
an informed teenager

From: Neil C. Reinhardt
E-mail was titled: "Religion sucks"

I am a 77 yr. old who is both much more experienced & more
knowledgeable than are most my age. I've traveled more, and done
so in more types of air craft, boats, trains and motor vehicles than
most.

I have been a deep sea diver and a Life-guard. Plus many other
things.

I have also worked for Magnavox, NCR and TRW as a manufacturing
supervisor and I was employed an as industrial engineer for
Xerox.

I served in the National Guard and/or Active Army Reserves for
over six years and in the regular army, mostly as a paratrooper in
the 101st Airborne for over three years. And I am an expert shot
who has fired many types of weapons, mortars, artillery 105s, 106's
RR and flame throwers.

I have Lived in more places, (3 countries, 10 states & 20 cities)
Lived at both higher and closer to the Atlantic (less than 80 feet)
and the Pacific (within 15 ft) than most. I've done more different
types of things than most people ever even think of doing, much
less actually do.

I've been an MP, taken law enforcement classes in college and I have been a Civil Defense Auxiliary Police officer.

AND, I have, MANY TIMES RISKED LIFE AND LIMB FOR OTHERS!

From doing so in the late 1950's and early 1960's for Black Civil Rights to the EIGHT Crimes, which as a private citizen, I have stopped in progress.

EXPERIENCE = KNOWLEDGE

THE MORE VARIED THE EXPERIENCE, THE MORE THE KNOWLEDGE GAINED My tested reading skills show I read, with high comprehension, at nearlydouble the speed of most college graduates, And my tested listening skills are four times better than ANY college graduates who had been tested up to that point in time,

My Gifted Level IQ places me in the top 2,5% and tests have proven I use my IQ nearly double as effectively as most use theirs,

While I have also tested to have above a PHD level Vocabulary, I seldom use it as using big words not only make one sound like a supercilious bibliophile, most cannot understand them anywho.

So I do what I can to assure that my communications meet the "Primary Purpose of Language" which means the successful communication of a desired message from me to one, or more others.

When this is accomplished, such things as incorrect grammar and/ or any misspelled words are of no importance. (FYI, Only the mentally challenged anal retentive nit pickers worry about such mundane things.)

As I also do the research to assure I have the facts to back me up, the odds of my being wrong on any subject I care to comment on are so close to zero they may well be zero.

SO, WHEN I TELL YOU SOMETHING IS A FACT, YOU CAN TAKE IT TO THE BANK!

I AM GOING TO PUT THE FOLLOWING IN SIMPLE LANGUAGE SO EVEN YOU ANTI-POT RETARDS CAN GRASP IT!

I HAVE STUDIED POT SINCE EARLY IN 1963 AND AFTER OVER A YEAR AND A HALF OF RESEARCH INTO IT. I HAVE OCCASIONALLY USED IN SINCE THE AROUND THE MIDDLE OF 1965.

YOU PEOPLE ARE A STUPID LYING PUNK RETARDS WHO HAVE YOUR HEADS UP YOUR A!? ABOUT MARIJUANA.

YOU WOULD NOT KNOW WHAT A FACT IS WHERE IT A VERY SHARP POINTED CACTUS SHOVED UP YOUR ASS UNTIL IT PROTRUDED FROM YOU IGNORANT MOUTHS!

YOU ARE LOW LIFE SCUM WHO CARE LESS ABOUT FACTS, OR ABOUT OTHERS

II IS TOO DAMN BAD YOU WERE NOT ABORTED!

Neil C. Reinhardt

A 77 year old Pro Iraq War Agnostic Atheist Activist, a former member of management in some of America's Top 500 corporations, 101st Airborne Vet.

A Truth Telling, Iconoclastic, Women Chasing-Catching, Philosophizing, Crime Stopping, Scuba and Deep Sea Diving, Fire Walking, Paratrooping, Life Saving, Spelunking, Lifeguarding, 1 & 3 Meter Spring Board Diving, Bungee Jumping, Partying and Dancing, Expert Shooting, Beach Volley Ball

Playing, and Grumpy Old 'Son Of A Beach!'

From: Neil Reinhardt through the e-mail of Neil C [NeilC@webtv. net]

Hi Thom,

I wrote this a while back.

Some TRUTH about MARIJUANA

While there are many kinds of people, they can be broken down into sub-sets of twos.

For instance, there are two types of people, those who think they know all there is to know.

And those who are very open-minded to the possibility there may be something they do not know about.

(Actually, the MORE you know, the more you realize how LITTLE you know.

So those who think they know it all, really know VERY, VERY little!)

Another two types are the ignorant and the stupid.

The facts are that ALL of us, every single one, ARE knowledgeable (or ignorant) of MANY, MANY things.

We are also ignorant of many things others are knowledgeable of and we are knowledgeable of things they are ignorant of.

Some stupid people cannot learn and they are not whom I referring to in this.

The difference between being ignorant and stupid is that ignorant people can learn and are willing to do so.

To me, the really stupid people are those who can learn and yet refuse to do so.

—

"Our minds are similar to a parachute in that for them to function properly, they must be fully open!

—

NCR Sez: MARIJUANA is NOT bad!

Science & many American's acknowledge this reality and it is FAR PAST time for our marijuana policies to reflect this fact.

When I was going to Mesa Junior College (in Grand Junction, Co.) I firmly believed all of the many bad things said about MARIJUANA.

I think I even wrote a report on it which espoused the lies about it I had learned up to that point in time.

After moving to Calif., I found that not only did many of the people who I met and really liked smoked it, as did one of my best friends mothers.

So I went out and did what most people do not do, I started researching it. I went to the library and started reading all I could on it.

After about a year and a half of talking to a lot of people who smoked and/or ate it, reading everything I could find on it, I concluded that I, and the rest of the American public, had been lied to.

I found it had been made illegal due to the perjured testimony of a senator and some others, as well the result of some "yellow" journalism by William Randolf Hurst.

Plus there was pressure from Dupont Chemical and the Mellon Bank. And from a very power hungry government official named Henry Armswinger.

I found the American Medical Association did NOT want marijuana made illegal as it already had PROVEN medical uses then (1935) and more to come.

I discovered it had been researched for OVER 400 years (this was in 1965) and that there was NOTHING wrong with it.

I found there was not ONE anti-marijuana study which had been conducted under the strict scientific guide lines such studies SHOULD be conducted under and that not ONE anti-marijuana study had been replicated by any other researcher.

So, I tried it.

Since I did not smoke, I, like President Clinton, did not inhale properly and so, I got NO effect from it.

After failing a few more times, I finally succeeded in inhaling properly and had a positive effect.

I have found that people get one of three effects from smoking and/ or eating Marijuana.

One, a very few people become paranoid.

Obliviously, they should NOT smoke or eat it.

(DUH!)

Two, it puts a few people to sleep.

So those people should only smoke and/or eat it when they want to go to sleep.

Three, MOST people get, like I did, a pleasurable effect from it.

I got to thinking about it and equate it to the following.

The original purpose of a car's muffler was to reduce the sound of the motor. And if you punch holes in the muffler, a truer sound of the motor will be emitted.

DO you hear your heart beating?

Do you hear yourself breathing?

NO, most people do not.

I submit we have a sort of muffler on our mind which reduces not only these sounds it also muffles other things as well.

You see, when marijuana effects me, the colors I see are more intense, the sounds have more clarity, food tastes better and my tactile enjoyment increases.

So I contend that the marijuana pokes holes in the muffler of my mind.

Tthen my mind experiences the true sensations of seeing, hearing, eating and feeling.

And logically, it really makes absolutely no difference if that is what really happens or not as IT IS what I perceive!

Next, do I give a darn what others may or may not think about my smoking and/or eating marijuana?

Heck no, it is none of their business!

If they want to be un-informed dodos, I could care less! If they do not want to enjoy what multi-millions of others do, it is fine with me.

———

Name: Luke
E-mail: lmorris7878@gmail.com

Message: I've watched a couple of American Weed episodes. I have no clue what has happened with the vote with the law that y'all have worked on passing, but the basic discussion on the legal growth and sell of marijuana is the topic of my e-mail.

I will start with me saying that I do not smoke marijuana, but my opinions on it differ on my choice not to smoke or ingest the plant. I live in South Carolina. My state prohibits the sale and ingestion of the drug, but it is actually easier to buy it than alcohol when you are not of age.

I would be lying if I were to say that "medical" marijuana is the sole reason for people that use the plant, and I'm sure that, at the heart of the matter, no one that sells it, or even doctors that issue the license, would say that they go through extensive medical testings in order to obtain the right to procure the drug. However, my argument focuses more on the initial, and historical, reason for the banning of the plant.

Since the 1930s, absolute cannabis use has been illegal (including the manufacture of hemp). While most debate why, most agree that it is due to business ties. DuPont started manufacturing Nylon, and those included in passing the law had business ties with DuPont. Hemp was cheaper to produce, which would obviously drive DuPont stocks down if allowed to compete. While this is a valid argument, I understand that hemp is not the argument; the effects of THC ingestion is what is to be contemplated.

I was not able to procure many sources and information on the abolition of THC, but I do know that it was in the early 20th century. Cigarettes—called Reefers, which is where the term comes from—were sold up to this point. Much like alcohol in the Abolition period, marijuana was demonized for it's effects on human decision making. Also, such as alcohol, people continued to produce and consume the product regardless of legal enforcement.

My argument questions your reasoning behind your opinion to the subject matter. Is it because it is the only thing you know to be true? If not, please explain why.

The illegality of marijuana does not prevent its sale or consumption (as exemplified in my state). Also, legalizing it raises prices—lowering (in theory) its consumption—brings in revenue in the form of taxes, and also lowers gang activity (if you are able to bring relevant statistics to the contrary, I am open to your ability to do so).

I also would like to address your use of children to even hold your signs. They cannot vote, therefore why include them in your campaign? I can respect your opinions, but your use of children to hold the signs of your opinion, then to tell those against you that they are picking on children while those opinions being carried are your own, and not necessarily their own? You are wrong, not only morally, but logically as well, and this is not disputable. You ask for them to pick on the adults, so here is myself "picking" on you. Answer my questions, without having children holding your retorts, and I will respond in the same respectful manner.

I look forward to hear your timely response.

Yours Truly,
Luke Morris

Name: Sarah
E-mail: sarahbaby420@live.com

Message: I was watching American weeds and heard ur interview on the grassroots radio station. what I heard was appalling. where did you get your stats from? because nothing you stated was close to being correct. marijuana is considerd a drug just like Vicodin, OxyContin, ect thousands of people die from these drugs and marijuana has been a track record of 0. hm . . . how does that make marijuana dangerous? oh yea it doesn't. and as for 6% of the patients need it is also incorrect, marijuana is replacing the use of pain killers which is good. marijuana makes people better just like Vicodin but with out the kidney and liver damage. I cannot say enough about how wrong and b!??!?!? all of your comments are about what makes marijuana bad. to be honest your ignorant about the subject. you obviously have not done your research and need to do so. marijuana is a natural safe medicine and is never going away so get use to it.

Name: Ryan
E-mail: ryanvandewater@yahoo.com

Message: Hope you enjoy having your town over run with real drug addicts and real crime with painkillers and meth. Good job guy

Name: David
E-mail: thecenturion@e-mail.com

Message: Hey Ray,

When did you decide that your true mission in life is making people endure needless suffering just because some arrogant selfish bastard like you has anointed himself to make personal choices for others?

Name: heather
E-mail: gabbigoo3509@gmail.com

Message: How can you live with yourself after telling such bold faced LIES! The "facts" you give are bogus and you should seriously ashamed if yourself. Instead of closing legal and regulated facilities, how about crack down on the ILLEGAL things that go on. Do you realize by banning it as you have it just puts it in criminal hands, forcing people to get it illegally and giving the money to CRIMINALS, instead of bringing money, jobs, and healing to the town you claim to love so much? Let me ask you, to you think doctors prescribing pain pills that can and do KILL people is better? Kids are dying everyday from that, people get hooked, kill their liver kidneys & bodies, yet that is ok? You should be ashamed of yourself. I don't even live in Colorado nor to I smoke marijuana but after seeing the show I am extremely disappointed in how you've behaved. Aren't there bigger fish to fry?!?!?! How sad you are!

Name: Dillon
E-mail: dillonyoung12@mybga.org

Message: Dear Mr. Martinez,

I am writing you concerning your opinions on the ban of medical marijuana dispensaries in Fort Collins, AZ. You may wish to note that I do not live in Fort Collins, nor Arizona for that matter, so there is little bias surrounding my opinion concerning the results of the Proposition. I would first like to tell you I believe your methods of getting your message across are peaceful, organized, and respectful. However, I feel you may not quite understand what the passing of Proposition 300 means. Do you understand that if the Proposition passes, then patients will just go to the black market for their marijuana needs? Wouldn't you rather have taxed, regulated, and safer locations selling marijuana to patients rather than patients turning to the black market? Proposition 300 does not criminalize marijuana, just the dispensaries. So why would you want to oppose dispensaries versus the black market? Thank you for your time.

Sincerely,
Dillon Young

Name: CHRISTOPHER JAMES CROMONIC
E-mail: CROMONIC@COMCAST.NET

Message: I JUST WATCHED WHAT YOU SAID ON THE SHOW ABOUT THE MEDICINE ISNT BROKEN DOWN INTO PERCENTS AND HOW THE BUDTENDERS DONT KNOW WHAT THEY ARE TALKIN BOUT, DO YOU EVEN WATCH THE SHOW, ITS GUYS LIKE YOU THAT WOULD RATHER HAVE THE MEXICAN CARTEL SELL POT FOR A HELL OF LOT CHEAPER THAN WHAT THE STORES DO AND, HAVE YOU EVER BEEN IN PAIN OR INJURED, IF YOU DIDNT THEN YOU HAVE NO IDEA WHAT PAIN IS LIKE, FOR MY SELF MARIJUANIA DOESNT FIX MY PAIN BUT THE PERCOCETS IM ON ISNT DOIN IT EITHER, SO WHAT DO YA WANT ME TO DO, DIE, LIVE IN PAIN, GIVE ME A BREAK AND STOP BEING SUCH A D!?! N A!? ABOUT THIS, ITS A PLANT NOT A DRUG FOR GODS SAKE, PULL THE STICK OUT OF YOUR A!? AND MAN UP. GO GET A JOB N DO SOMETHING BESIDES TALKIN LIKE A MORON EVERY TIME YOU ARE ON THE

AIR CUZ YOU SOUND LIKE SUCH A OLD TIME DUMBA!?,
W T F,

Name: Whit
E-mail: whitwarren007@gmail.com

Message: Why are you trying to take away a natural, harmless medicine from ailing patients and force them to use man made medicine with tons, TONS more side effects? You disgust me. Get your facts straight before you start spreading straight LIES.

Name: jeffrey
E-mail: jeffreynascar@aol.com

Message: It's clear array that when you were in school you probably told home everybody. All I can hope is someone in your family has a death stricken illness. In the only thing that makes them feel better is pot. Whether it be your wife children or parents. And if pot was the only thing that made him feel better what would you do. You have gone from class tattletale, to the towns tattletale. Good for you you told on people your whole life. See you own the show you rat. Wipe the shit off your nose.

Name: we know you sold your soul
E-mail: weknowyousoldyoursoul@devil.com

Message: you are a liar! and a dumb A!? and a retard and i know you will burn in hell . . . . btw you deserve it

Name: Karina
E-mail: kllg222@hotmail.com

Message: Hi my name is Karina, I was watching the program american weed, and I feel proud that we have people like you that really protect the community, I live in Colorado Springs, so Im very tier to see everywhere this dispenseries, I have friends that they are very involve in this industrie, but still I against marihuana because no matter what still a drug, and because of many people that they grow maarihuana in there houses kids have more access to this drug and take to schools and share with other kids, also many kids now help their parents to trim these plants, and we are talking about kids around 10-14 years old, I know this industrie make money to the city but I don't like the price that we have to pay for that, we are stilling the inocence of our kids, and know they are becoming a consumers at very short age, I wish you would be here to close all this dispensaries, because here I don't see any body do anything for it, and if you know people in Colorado Springs working to fix this problem, please let me know, I would appreciate very much and help them to clean our city, I think you are a hope for me and for many other people thank you very much.

Sincerely Karina

PS. Im sorry for my grammar, English is my second languege, thank you againg.

In my replies to the e-mails, regardless of how disrespectful they were, the following message was sent:

"I don't think anyone is against its medical use (legitimate use) done through the FDA, like all other drugs with a doctor's prescription. So we are in agreement there . . .

Here is more information for you . . ."

John A. Howard, Ph.D.

Senior Fellow the Howard Center on Family, Religion, and Society Member of the National Commission on Marijuana and Drug Abuse (1971-73)

In September of 1998, Current Concerns,[2] a periodical published in Zurich, Switzerland, printed a statement by Professor Henri Baylon, President of the French National Academy of Medicine. It includes excerpts from the general conclusions arrived at in the 1992 International Colloquium on Illegal Drugs co-sponsored by the National Academy of Medicine and the City of Paris. Among those conclusions: "The harmfulness of cannabis (marijuana) is very well documented today, experimentally and clinically. This drug damages the central nervous system, the lungs, the immunological resistance and the reproduction functions . . . It is absolutely essential to start an information and prevention campaign which takes into consideration the legal as well as the health risks of using cannabis."

William Buckley claims that nobody has ever been found dead of marijuana. As one physician has remarked, "Saying no one ever died from smoking marijuana is like saying no one ever died from smoking tobacco." The April 2003 issue of the Australian Family Association's newsletter[1] provides its current report on cannabis-related deaths: 184 in Australia, 664 in the United States in 1999 (reported by the Drug Abuse Warning Network) and six cannabis-related cardiovascular deaths in Norway.

Chronic cannabis smoking can produce sinusitis, pharyngitis, bronchitis, emphysema, and other respiratory difficulties in a year or less, as opposed to ten to twenty years of cigarette smoking to produce comparable complications. (Dr. Forest Tennant Jr., officer-in-charge of the Drug Abuse Program for the U. S. Army Europe, 1971-72; Dr. William T. Moore, associate professor of Clinical Psychiatry, University of Pennsylvania School of Medicine).

So do we keep adding healthcare costs in the future with the influence on children—thinking "it's OK to do because look at all of the marijuana stores in Fort Collins?" Dr. Wison of PSD already reported the significant impact it is having in their schools.

Dr. D. Harvey Powelson was asked what he would say to high school kids if he had the opportunity . . . He replied: "That it damages the brain, that it damages your ability to think, it damages your chromosomes, it damages your immunity system—all of this at the rate of something i the neighborhood of twenty times as rapidly as alcohol."

Dr. Powelson was once quoted in the *Daily Californian* as saying, "Marijuana is harmless. There is no evidence that it does anything except make people feel good. It has never made anyone into a criminal or a narcotics addict. It should be legalized." But now he is widely quoted as the psychiatrist who has reversed his opinion on legalization of marijuana. What changed his mind was the intensive research he completed, and in the course of his work, either directly or indirectly, he saw literally thousands of students. Dr. Powelson was formerly chief of the psychiatry department of Cowell Memorial Hospital at the University of California at Berkeley.

On September 18, 2002, the *New York Times* printed the following as a full-page ad, "An Open Letter To Parents About Marijuana." The text begins,

"Marijuana puts kids at risk. It is the most widely used illicit drug among youth today and is more potent than ever. Marijuana use can lead to a host of significant health, social, learning, and behavioral problems at a crucial time in a young person's development . . . And don't be fooled by popular beliefs. Kids can get hooked on pot. Research shows that marijuana can lead to addiction. More teens enter treatment for marijuana abuse each year than for all other illicit drugs combined."

The ad is signed by eighteen organizations. Among them are American Academy of Family Physicians, American Academy of Pediatrics, American College of Emergency Physicians, American Medical Association, American Society of Addiction Medicine, Child Welfare League of America, National Center for School Health Nursing, National Medical Association, and the National Parent Teachers Association.

Below on government report:

"Medical" Marijuana—The Facts

Medical marijuana already exists. It's called Marinol. A pharmaceutical product, Marinol is widely available through prescription. It comes in the form of a pill and is also being studied by researchers for suitability via other delivery methods, such as an inhaler or patch. The active ingredient of Marinol is synthetic THC, which has been found to relieve the nausea and vomiting associated with chemotherapy for cancer patients and to assist with loss of appetite with AIDS patients.

Unlike smoked marijuana—which contains more than four different chemicals, including most of the hazardous chemicals found in tobacco smoke—Marinol has been studied and approved by the medical community and the Food and Drug Administration (FDA), the nation's watchdog over unsafe and harmful food and drug products. Since the passage of the 1906 Pure Food and Drug Act, any drug that is marketed in the United States must undergo rigorous scientific testing. The approval process mandated by this act ensures that claims of safety and therapeutic value are supported by clinical evidence and keeps unsafe, in effective and dangerous drugs off the market.

There are no FDA-approved medications that are smoked. For one thing, smoking is generally a poor way to deliver medicine. It is difficult to administer safe, regulated dosages of medicines in smoked form. Secondly, the harmful chemicals and carcinogens that are byproducts of smoking create entirely new health problems. There are four times the levels of tar in a marijuana cigarette, for example, than in a tobacco cigarette.

Morphine, for example, has proven to be a medically valuable drug, but the FDA does not endorse the smoking of opium or heroin. Instead, scientists have extracted active ingredients from opium, which are sold as pharmaceutical products like morphine, codeine, hydrocodone, or oxycodone. In a similar vein, the FDA has not approved smoking marijuana for medicinal purposes but has approved the active ingredient—THC—in the form of scientifically regulated Marinol.

The DEA helped facilitate the research on Marinol. The National Cancer Institute approached the DEA in the early 1980s regarding their study of THC's in relieving nausea and vomiting. As a result, the DEA facilitated the registration and provided regulatory support and guidance for the study.

The DEA recognizes the importance of listening to science. That's why the DEA has registered seven research initiatives to continue researching the effects of smoked marijuana as medicine. For example, under one program established by the State of California, researchers are studying the potential use of marijuana and its ingredients on conditions such as multiple sclerosis and pain. At this time, however, neither the medical community nor the scientific community has found sufficient data to conclude that smoked marijuana is the best approach to dealing with these important medical issues.

The most comprehensive, scientifically rigorous review of studies of smoked marijuana was conducted by the Institute of Medicine, an organization chartered by the National Academy of Sciences. In a report released in 1999, the institute did not recommend the use of smoked marijuana but did conclude that active ingredients in marijuana could be isolated and developed into a variety of pharmaceuticals, such as Marinol. In the meantime, the DEA is working with pain-management groups, such as Last Acts, to make sure that those who need access to safe, effective pain medication can get the best medication available.

For those who reason, "Hey, I smoked some weed when I was growing up and it did not hurt me," let me offer this. Most of us grew up in a time when there were no child car seats and almost no one wore seat belts and "Hey, we're all still here!" Did we use that logic to justify not protecting our kids in child car seats and seat belts? Thirty-some years later, we continue to learn more and more detrimental effects of marijuana. Should we protect our children and grandchildren from those like we do from unnecessary injuries from car crashes?

The evidence shows that sanctioned legal distribution of marijuana in our state increases marijuana usage by our youth. As a conscientious, health-conscious community, shouldn't we make decisions for future generations that will reflect those values?

Alcohol tax collected nationwide is $14.5B, but the social and health cost is $185B. The smoking tax collected $25B, however, the social cost us $200B (Colorado sheriffs, Colorado Drug Investigators Assoc., ONDCP Director Gil Kerlikowske statement, March 4, 2010).

I care about the seriously ill, and I also care about the health of our youth. We cannot afford the social cost and ramifications of our young adults' future by closing our eyes to the truth being undermined. Next we will see other habit-forming drugs being considered as medicine through popular votes instead of the FDA.

The heavy marketing that you see today is only the beginning. We never see doctors and pharmacists doing sign dancing on our streets promoting drugs. Pharmacies don't entice a person to take drugs through tantalizing candy wrappers that simulate other popular brands of candy. Let's be honest, the intent is wrong, and it is up to us to correct it and bring out the truth.

Sheriff's Office seizure after arrests for armed robbery of MMD store in Fort Collins.

Picture courtesy of the Larimer County Sheriff's Office

Marijuana NIDA

Marijuana is the most commonly abused illicit drug in the United States. It is a dry, shredded green-and-brown mix of flowers, stems, seeds, and leaves derived from the hemp plant cannabis sativa. The main active chemical in marijuana is delta-9 tetrahydrocannabinol; THC for short.

How is Marijuana Abused?

Marijuana is usually smoked as a cigarette (joint) or in a pipe. It is also smoked in blunts, which are cigars that have been emptied of tobacco and refilled with marijuana. Since the blunt retains the tobacco leaf used to wrap the cigar, this mode of delivery combines marijuana's active ingredients with nicotine and other harmful chemicals. Marijuana can also be mixed in food or brewed as a tea. As a more concentrated, resinous form, it is called hashish, and as a sticky black liquid, hash oil. Marijuana smoke has a pungent and distinctive, usually sweet-and-sour odor.

How Does Marijuana Affect the Brain?

Scientists have learned a great deal about how THC acts in the brain to produce its many effects. When someone smokes marijuana, THC rapidly passes from the lungs into the bloodstream, which carries the chemical to the brain and other organs throughout the body.

THC acts upon specific sites in the brain, called cannabinoid receptors, kicking off a series of cellular reactions that ultimately lead to the high that users experience when they smoke marijuana. Some brain areas have many cannabinoid receptors; others have few or none. The highest density of cannabinoid receptors are found in parts of the brain that influence pleasure, memory, thoughts, concentration, sensory and time perception, and coordinated movement.[1]

Not surprisingly, marijuana intoxication can cause distorted perceptions, impaired coordination, difficulty in thinking and problem solving, and problems with learning and memory. Research has shown that marijuana's adverse impact on learning and memory can last for days or weeks after the acute effects of the drug wear off.[2] As a result, someone who smokes marijuana every day may be functioning at a suboptimal intellectual level all of the time.

Research on the long-term effects of marijuana abuse indicates some changes in the brain similar to those seen after long-term abuse of other major drugs. For example, cannabinoid withdrawal in chronically exposed animals leads to an increase in the activation of the stress-response system[3] and changes in the activity of nerve cells containing dopamine.[4] Dopamine neurons are involved in the regulation of motivation and reward and are directly or indirectly affected by all drugs of abuse.

Addictive Potential [5]

Long-term marijuana abuse can lead to addiction; that is, compulsive drug seeking and abuse despite its known harmful effects upon social functioning in the context of family, school, work, and recreational activities. Long-term marijuana abusers trying to quit report irritability, sleeplessness, decreased appetite, anxiety, and drug craving, all of which make it difficult to quit. These withdrawal symptoms begin within about one day following abstinence, peak at two to three days, and subside within one or two weeks following drug cessation.

Marijuana and Mental Health

A number of studies have shown an association between chronic marijuana use and increased rates of anxiety, depression, suicidal ideation, and schizophrenia. Some of these studies have shown age at first use to be a factor, where early use is a marker of vulnerability to later problems. However, at this time, it is not clear whether marijuana use causes mental problems, exacerbates them, or is used in attempt to self-medicate symptoms already in existence. Chronic marijuana use, especially in a very young person, may also be a marker of risk for mental illnesses, including addiction, stemming from genetic or environmental vulnerabilities, such as early exposure to stress or violence. At the present time, the strongest evidence links marijuana use and schizophrenia and/or related disorders.[6] High doses of marijuana can produce an acute psychotic reaction; in addition, use of the drug may trigger the onset or relapse of schizophrenia in vulnerable individuals.

What Other Adverse Effect Does Marijuana Have on Health?

Effects on the Heart

Marijuana increases heart rate by 20to 100 percent shortly after smoking; this effect can last up to three hours. In one study, it was estimated that marijuana users have a 4.8-fold increase in the risk of heart attack in the first hour after smoking the drug.[7] This may be due to the increased heart rate as well as effects of marijuana on heart rhythms, causing palpitations and arrhythmias. This risk may be greater in aging populations or those with cardiac vulnerabilities.

Effects on the Lungs

Numerous studies have shown marijuana smoke to contain carcinogens and to be an irritant to the lungs. In fact, marijuana smoke contains 50 to70 percent more carcinogenic hydrocarbons than does tobacco smoke. Marijuana users usually inhale more deeply and hold their breath longer than tobacco smokers do, which further increase the lungs' exposure to carcinogenic smoke. Marijuana smokers show deregulated growth of epithelial cells in their lung tissue, which could lead to cancer;[8] however, a recent case-controlled study found no positive associations between marijuana use and lung, upper respiratory, or upper digestive-tract cancers.[9] Thus, the link between marijuana smoking and these cancers remains unsubstantiated at this time.

Nonetheless, marijuana smokers can have many of the same respiratory problems as tobacco smokers, such as daily cough and phlegm production, more frequent acute chest illness, and a heightened risk of lung infections. A study of 450 individuals found that people who smoke marijuana frequently but do not smoke tobacco have more health problems and miss more days of work than nonsmokers.[10] Many of the extra sick days among the marijuana smokers in the study were for respiratory illnesses.

Effects on Daily Life

Research clearly demonstrates that marijuana has the potential to cause problems in daily life or make a person's existing problems worse. In one study, heavy marijuana abusers reported that the drug impaired several important measures of life achievement including physical and mental health, cognitive abilities, social life, and career status.[11] Several studies associate workers' marijuana smoking with increased absences, tardiness, accidents, workers' compensation claims, and job turnover.

What Treatment Options Exist?

Behavioral interventions, including cognitive behavioral therapy and motivational incentives (i.e., providing vouchers for goods or services to patients who remain abstinent) have shown efficacy in treating marijuana dependence. Although no medications are currently available, recent discoveries about the workings of the cannabinoid system offer promise for the development of medications to ease withdrawal, block the intoxicating effects of marijuana, and prevent relapse.

The latest treatment data indicate that in 2006, marijuana was the most common illicit drug of abuse and was responsible for about 16 percent (289,988) of all admissions to treatment facilities in the United States. Marijuana admissions were primarily male (73.8 percent), white (51.5 percent), and young (36.1 percent were in the fifteen-to-nineteen age range). Those in treatment for primary marijuana abuse had begun use at an early age: 56.2 percent had abused it by age fourteen and 92.5 percent had abused it by age eighteen.

How Widespread is Marijuana Abuse?

According to the National Survey on Drug Use and Health (NSDUH), in 2007, 14.4 million Americans aged twelve or older used marijuana at least once in the month prior to being surveyed, which is similar to the 2006 rate. About six thousand people a day in 2007 used marijuana for the first time—2.1 million Americans. Of these, 62.2 percent were under age eighteen.

Monitoring the Future Survey

The Monitoring the Future survey indicates that marijuana use among eight, tenth, and twelfth graders—which has shown a consistent decline since the mid-1990s—appears to have leveled off, with 10.9 percent of eighth graders, 23.9 percent of tenth graders, and 32.4 percent of twelfth graders reporting past-year use. Heightening the concern over this stabilization in use is the finding that, compared to last year, the proportion of eighth graders who perceived smoking marijuana as harmful and the proportion who disapprove of the drug's use have decreased.

Chapter 16 Endnotes

1. Herkenham M, Lynn A, Little MD, et al. Cannabinoid receptor localization in the brain. Proc Natl Acad Sci, USA 87(5):1932-1936, 1990.
2. Pope HG, Gruber AJ, Hudson JI, Huestis MA, Yurgelun-Todd D. Neuropsychological performance in long-term cannabis users. Arch Gen Psychiatry 58(10):909-915, 2001.
3. Rodríguez de Fonseca F, Carrera MRA, Navarro M, Koob GF, Weiss F. Activation of corticotropin-releasing factor in the limbic system during cannabinoid withdrawal. Science 276(5321):2050-2054, 1997.
4. Diana M, Melis M, Muntoni AL, Gessa GL. Mesolimbic dopaminergic decline after cannabinoid withdrawal. Proc Natl Acad Sci, USA 95(17):10269-10273, 1998.
5. Budney AJ, Vandrey RG, Hughes JR, Thostenson JD, Bursac Z. Comparison of cannabis and tobacco withdrawal: Severity and contribution to relapse. J Subst Abuse Treat, e-publication ahead of print, March 12, 2008.
6. Moore TH, Zammit S, Lingford-Hughes A, et al. Cannabis use and risk of psychotic or affective mental health outcomes: A systematic review. Lancet 370 (9584):319-328, 2007.
7. Mittleman MA, Lewis RA, Maclure M, Sherwood JB, Muller JE. Triggering myocardial infarction by marijuana. Circulation 103(23):2805-2809, 2001.
8. Tashkin DP. Smoked marijuana as a cause of lung injury. Monaldi Arch Chest Dis 63(2):92-100, 2005.
9. Hashibe M, Morgenstern H, Cui Y, et al. Marijuana use and the risk of lung and upper aerodigestive tract cancers: Results of a population-based case-control study. Cancer Epidemiol Biomarkers Prev 15(10):1829-1834, 2006.
10. Polen MR, Sidney S, Tekawa IS, Sadler M, Friedman GD. Health care use by frequent marijuana smokers who do not smoke tobacco. West J Med 158(6):596-601, 1993.
11. Gruber AJ, Pope HG, Hudson JI, Yurgelun-Todd D. Attributes of long-term heavy cannabis users: A case control study. Psychological Med 33(8):1415-1422, 2003.

CHAPTER 17

Other Perspectives

Below is a letter sent to me via e-mail by Ray Spitzer of Glendale, AZ.

I've undertaken an attack on the proponents of medical marijuana in Arizona. This state passed an initiative allowing medical marijuana in 2010. Thus far, the dispensaries have not been allowed to open because the Republicans have been fighting it under federal law threats or perceived threats. I sent a copy of the following to the legislators in Arizona, asking them to wake up and get an initiative on the ballot to kill this lie of medical marijuana. If any of it helps you, great.

Medical Marijuana is an Oxymoron

While in the military I was given a collateral duty. I was to be one of a few people who would be a Drug and Alcohol Education Specialists (DAES). I spent two months in school—about 320 hours—learning the pharmacology of all the drugs known at the time, as well as everything possible to understand about the effects of alcohol. It was, to say the least, a very enlightening two months. Once that school was over, I was then the identified specialist at every command where I was serving. I've heard every excuse for using drugs and abusing alcohol that can be manufactured. I have also worked as a volunteer inside two state prisons, and one paid position as a computer instructor in a federal prison. In the state prisons I worded for a prison ministry, assisting convicts who had proven that they wanted to turn their lives around. Between the one-on-one sessions, and general interaction with about 80 convicts, about 75 of them were in prison for offenses that involved drugs and alcohol. I also worked as a volunteer, serving on a Foster Care Review

Board for two years, and four years as a court-appointed advocate for kids in foster care. Between the prison experiences and the foster care experiences, I again heard just about every excuse possible for using meth, alcohol, crack, heroin, marijuana, PCP, you name it.

Anyone who tells you that marijuana is "medicine" is lying to you. There is absolutely no scientific evidence that marijuana contains any medicinal qualities. Arizona passed the Medical Marijuana initiative in 2010, though it still has not started operating in any meaningful way. There are questions about whether the vote was somehow rigged since it took so long for the final vote was released, but that's another story. What I'm suggesting to you is that you ask anyone who wants medical marijuana the following questions.

1. If medical marijuana is medicine, why has not it been submitted to the FDA for approval?
2. If medical marijuana is medicine, why aren't doctors prescribing its use? What we see are some doctors who sell recommendations for use, for a hefty fee.
3. California has had medical marijuana as a lawful enterprise for some time, and it's a nightmare. In general, the users of medical marijuana are in the 18-30 age groups. Why is that?
4. Medical marijuana dispensaries sell marijuana under literally dozens of names. If medical marijuana is medicine, why are there so many names for medical marijuana? If different kinds of medical marijuana contains varying levels of "medicine," shouldn't the doctor "recommended" that I take medical marijuana tell me which brand to use, how often, and how much per dose? Wouldn't medical marijuana be the same for all? Help, I'm confused.
5. What is the name of the so-called medicine in medical marijuana? It cannot be THC. THC is an acknowledged hallucinogen—it gets you stoned. So what is the medical ingredient in medical marijuana, and how much of it do I need?
6. When someone buys medical marijuana, do they receive a label on the container that tells them what the proper dose is, how many doses to take each day, and any possible side effects, like hallucinations, urge to eat snacks, sleepiness?

7. If I roll my own marijuana cigarettes, how much medical marijuana should I put into each marijuana cigarette? If I eat marijuana cupcakes or cookies, how much marijuana should be contained in each cupcake or cookie?

8. If I am smoking medical marijuana, is it legal for me to drive a car or operate machinery? If so, since its medicine, if I have an accident and destroy property, or kill someone, is the taking of medical marijuana a legitimate defense?

9. If I take marijuana and go to work, and while there I cause an accident because my judgment is impaired, and a person get hurt or killed, is the use of medical marijuana a legitimate defense?

10. If I have a medical marijuana card, can I smoke my medicine at work or on company property, even though cigarette smokers cannot?

11. If I were somehow arrested for a crime and sent to jail or prison, and I possess a medical marijuana card, does the jail or prison have to give me my medical marijuana since it is medical marijuana?

12. If I'm at home, consuming my medical marijuana, and somehow cause a fire that destroys my apartment building, is my possession of a medical marijuana card a legitimate defense?

13. If I'm a student attending college, and I need my "medicine," can I light up a marijuana cigarette and smoke it inside a building or classroom, or outside? I know smoking of cigarettes is illegal on college campuses, but how about the smoking of medical marijuana?

14. If I'm a police officer, member of the FBI, DEA, CIA, a Congressman, or President, can I take my medical marijuana while on the job? I mean, after all, it is medicine, isn't it?

15. If I'm a commercial pilot, can I take my medical marijuana while I flying an aircraft with 200 or 300 passengers onboard? I mean, after all, it is medicine.

Ladies and gentlemen, medical marijuana is an absolute lie. If you were to ask the questions I listed above to any of the advocates of medical marijuana, they would run away from you so fast you'd see a vapor trail. It's nothing but a ruse to get marijuana into the mainstream and it's wrong. Marijuana consumption affects your memory, affects brain cells, can cause serious medical problems. They call it medicine because when you consume it, by whatever means, the THC gets you "high," and you don't feel the pain as much. That's not medicine by any reasonable definition. People say that OxyCodone, Vicadin, Percocet, and other pain killers don't work for them, but at least you know what's in them. When you go into a medical marijuana dispensary, there are dozens of different kinds of marijuana in jars, all with catchy little names. You know what the difference is? The amount of THC they "think" they contain, and they sell for different prices to boot.

For those people who voted for medical marijuana in their state, you've been fooled, badly. It's a lie.

Ray Spitzer
Glendale, AZ

Anonymous citizen comment:

"I really would like someone to explain to us voters how such a thing can legally be put on our state ballot—to openly flaunt a known Federal law. The logic escapes me. Amendment 20 is not really valid, since it violates Federal law, too. Aren't we a nation that respects the law? I wish I was a lawyer."

Anonymous citizen comment:

Hi, Ray,

Well it looks like we have met somewhere in the middle. The problem is that some medical issues are not physical; it can be used to effectively treat bi-polar disorder and some anxiety disorders. However, you are exactly right. It should be controlled, and it should be controlled in a safer environment. Dispensaries are not safe. They should be more of a clinical atmosphere where there is a pharmaceutical environment, and the medication can be stored in a secure area. The FDA should be involved, and so should the APA.

We are years from completely understanding the long-term effects of the THC, but at least we can begin legitimate studies. I would volunteer for a scientific study, if there were no incriminating elements.

Dear Ray,

We have not met. I had the privilege of seeing you tonight on the National Geographic channel in the show "American Weed."

I just want to applaud you for your forthrightness, honesty, sincerity, and factual correctness, on the issue of dispensing marijuana, that isn't medical at all. It is plain and simple pushing drugs for profit.

As a charter member of the *Society for the Prevention of Drug Pushing Profits*, I appreciate your dedication and hard work in eradicating illegal drugs, like marijuana. It is a federal offense.

It was interesting to watch how marijuana cultivators grow marijuana in open areas where school kids have access to it, and also note how marijuana dispensaries set up shop near schools so that they can get kids hooked on drugs, thereby increasing their profits.

In fact, I read that the Boulder County District Attorney is protecting marijuana dispensaries close to schools, telling the United States Attorney for Colorado not to prosecute them federally because it is a Boulder issue.

CHAPTER 18

A Small Town Problem

We often do not think that small rural communities or towns are impacted by the misleading information about drugs. In this chapter, Officer Jeremy Yachik, drug enforcement officer for the Berthoud Police Department in Colorado, shares his opinion with me along with a public report that he prepared for the chief of police, Glenn Johnson. Officer Yachik contributed the following personal statement based on his law enforcement experience:

"I was hired on in Berthoud in December of 2007. Previously I was with the Las Animas County Sheriff's Office and the Trinidad Police Department. During my time in Berthoud I have seen criminal cases regarding the illicit use of marijuana sky rocket and I can pinpoint exactly when the trend began.

In March 2009 Attorney General Eric Holder stated that the Justice Department would only target "Medical" Marijuana providers who violate both federal AND state law. Subsequently the headline in The New York Times read *Obama Administration to Stop Raids on Medical Marijuana Dispensers*. After that, so-called "Medical" Marijuana Dispensaries started popping up all over Colorado. Just in Berthoud alone we had seven at one time; seven dispensaries for a rural town of 5,500 people. I remember thinking to myself, seven dispensaries, how many farmers smoke weed?

While these dispensaries were open incidents with Juveniles in possession of marijuana increased exponentially. Over the next 2 years we saw marijuana related calls at the local High School increase by 500%. We even started having contacts where Middle School aged kids were smoking marijuana and we began getting reports from the local Middle School, something we had not seen before.

One of the most disturbing trends I noticed was the amount of juveniles that were contacted for marijuana and simply did not care. They would say "Its medical" or "its medicine so it can't be bad." Funny thing is I have heard several kids use this line before when referencing the abuse of prescription medicines. I remember having one kid tell me that I could arrest him over and over because he was not going to stop because it "medicine".

In 1982 Nancy Regan uttered the phrase "Just say no" when asked by a student what to do if she was offered drugs, I was 6 years old. I remember all through school being taught to Just Say No. I watched my older brother ruin his life and his family with Meth and other drugs, starting with marijuana, and all I could ever think was to Just Say No. Where did that all go? I was scared to death of drugs, including marijuana; I would have never tried drugs in middle school or high school. The fact that Society has shied away from the fact that Marijuana is a Schedule I substance for a reason is an atrocity. It is setting up our future generations for failure.

During the time the dispensaries have been open we saw an increase in criminal cases. There have been cases of juveniles in possession of "medical" marijuana from the dispensaries. There has been a 160% increase in the amount of DUIs involving marijuana and most have been "medical" marijuana related. We have had a dispensary take stolen property in exchange for marijuana. We have had a dispensary broken into by 18 year olds attempting to steal marijuana. We have had 2 individuals, one a dispensary manager, gather over a pound of marijuana from several dispensaries and attempt to sell it to an undercover Officer that they though was 17.

I have contacted people that say by having "Medical" Marijuana legalized we take out the black market, they are gravely mistaken. We have seen an increase in the black market especially to juveniles. What I have seen is people over 18 with Medical Marijuana Card buy marijuana from a dispensary at $15 a gram and turns around and sells it to juveniles for $20-$25 a gram. Some may say "a gram isn't that much" but when you consider that the marijuana is now consistently 30% THC or better, as compared to marijuana of the 70's that was at most 5%, you are looking at 1 gram that equals the potency of 6 grams. Given the high potency of the "Medical" grade marijuana there has even been an increase in the amount of patients being seen at the local area Hospitals for side effects of Marijuana.

If anyone is on the fence about supporting medical marijuana, I implore you to simply *Just Say No*."

The following is the Berthoud Police public report of the impact that the MMDs had on their community; it is astounding.

BERTHOUD POLICE DEPARTMENT
328 MASSACHUSETTS AVE., P.O. BOX 1229
BERTHOUD, COLORADO 80513

PH: 970-532-2611   FAX: 970-532-3534

Medical Marijuana and its impact on crime in Berthoud.

The facts contained within this report were taken directly from Berthoud Police Department cases spanning 2 years 4 months before and after November 2009 when the dispensary known as Herb's Medicinals opened at 435 Mountain Ave. Other dispensaries in Town were open at that time and some of the stats include those Dispensaries however, Herb's Medicinals is now the only Dispensary open in Berthoud.

The statistics only include cases where marijuana, medical or not, were directly involved. The statistics labeled specifically as medicinal marijuana are only based on facts leading the reasonable person to believe that the marijuana came from a dispensary or is in possession of a medical marijuana card holder. Cases where the marijuana is of medical grade but not factually related to a dispensary or medical marijuana are simply counted as marijuana.

Statistical Data

These statistics were derived by comparison of the cases reported after Herb's Medicinals opened to the cases before they opened. This was done to illustrate the effect Medical Marijuana on the crime rate in Berthoud.

Category	% +/-
Total cases involving marijuana	+ 57%
Marijuana reports from Berthoud High School	+ 500%
Juvenile marijuana reports. (Juveniles in possession of marijuana and/or paraphernalia)	+ 94%
Adult marijuana reports. (Adults in possession of marijuana and/or paraphernalia)	+ 76%
Drug endangered children involving marijuana	0% *
Driving under the influence of drugs, specifically marijuana	+ 160%

* There were the same number of drug endangered children cases before and after the dispensary opened however, all the drug endangered children cases after the dispensary opened were Medical Marijuana related.

Prior to the dispensary opening there were no cases like the following reported therefore it is impossible to formulate a percentage.

Category	# of Cases
Medical Marijuana related cases	29
Marijuana cases reported at Turner Middle School	1
Juvenile DUI/D *, specifically marijuana	3
Juvenile DUI/D, specifically medicinal marijuana	1
Adults DUI/D, specifically medical marijuana	7
Juveniles in possession of medical marijuana	5
Drug endangered children cases related to medical marijuana	3
Drug endangered children involved in a DUI/D involving medical marijuana	1

* DUI/D- Driving under the influence of drugs.

Summaries of cases involving Medical Marijuana directly related to Herb's Medicinals.

Case # 2010-132

During an undercover investigation James Vester, the then manager of Herb's Medicinals was charged along with Daniel Gruber for attempting to sell one pound of marijuana to an Undercover Officer they believed to be 17 years old. The entire deal was done over text messages and Gruber made several comments stating that they could get all the medicinal grade marijuana wanted. The marijuana confiscated in the search warrant was packaged in labeled bags consistent with Medical Marijuana Dispensary packaging. 10 plants were also located along with a firearm and other drugs. Vester and Gruber were both convicted for Contributing to the Delinquency of a Minor.

Case # 2010-515 & 2010-542

A report was received and investigated by the Berthoud Police Department about rare and valuable coins that were stolen from the a residence. A report was later received and investigated that the residents believed they knew who had stolen the coins. Upon investigation it was determined who had stolen the items from the residents and they used the coins to purchase marijuana from Kevin Ballinger at Herb's Medicinals. It was discovered that Ballinger did not take the coins at face value but instead gave the suspect $120.00 of marijuana from the Dispensary for the coins. When questioned, Ballinger admitted to the transaction and turned over the coins to the Berthoud Police Department. Ballinger stated that he thought the coins were stolen and contacted the suspect's mother who stated that the coins were not hers but that the suspect sometimes gets stuff from a female friend. Upon questioning the suspect he stated that his friends which he identified would regularly pick him up and, because he was a Medical Marijuana Licensee, they would take him to Herb's Medicinals where the friends would give him money to purchase medical marijuana for them. The suspect stated that he would buy the marijuana and split it with his friends that were not Medical Marijuana Licensees. Charges against Ballinger were not accepted by the DA's Office because he made an attempt to verify the validity of the coins ownership.

Case # 11-47

Individuals were contacted in the Hays parking lot and marijuana was located in the vehicle. The bag had a Herb's Medicinals label on it. The Driver showed physiological signs of being under the influence of marijuana. The driver and the passenger were NOT Medical Marijuana Licensees and claimed that they got the marijuana from a friend that was.

Case # 2011-89

Two males broke entry into Herb's Medicinals and attempted to steal marijuana. Upon identification of the suspects they admitted to their involvement and stated that the goal of the burglary was not money but marijuana. Both suspects were charged and convicted. Both suspects were 18 years old.

Summaries of cases involving Medical Marijuana NOT directly related to Herb's Medicinals.

Case # 2009-647   Dispensary: Natural Alternative Pain Management

During a response to answer Dispensary Owner questions about Medical Marijuana it was discovered that the dispensary was selling product not grown or made by the Dispensary Owners. At the time it was only "legal" to be a caregiver or a patient. If you were a caregiver then you must grow the patient's marijuana for them and can then make edibles for the patient. Therefore, the Dispensary Owner turned over approximately 19 grams of "Purple Nurple" marijuana and 33 THC suckers to the Berthoud Police Department to be destroyed.

Natural Alternative Pain Management closed shortly after this incident.

Case # 2010-90   Dispensary: Unknown

During a suspicious vehicle stop 5 bags of marijuana were found in the vehicle. Several of the bags were labeled with the marijuana strain names "Blueberry" and "Train Wreck" as well as the weights. A scale was also located with the marijuana. The driver subsequently confessed to selling marijuana and stated the marijuana was acquired by a "friend" that had a medical marijuana card from an unknown dispensary.

Case # 2010-92   Dispensary: Medicine Man Medical Marijuana Dispensary

An Officer responded to a report of an individual smoking marijuana in a vehicle parked in front of the Medicine Man Medical Marijuana Dispensary. Upon contact the Officer observed a male sitting in the Driver's seat smoking a marijuana cigarette. The male surrendered the marijuana to the Officer and stated that he had a Medical Marijuana License that had expired.

The Medicine Man Medical Marijuana Dispensary closed shortly after this incident.

Case # 2010-106   Dispensary: Unknown

During a vehicle stop Officers arrested the Driver for DUI/D. The marijuana found in the vehicle belonged to a passenger who was a Medical Marijuana Licensee. The Driver was not Medical Marijuana Licensee.

Case # 2010-152   Dispensary: Unknown Denver Area

During a vehicle stop the Officer arrested the Driver for DUI/D. During the contact the Driver admitted to being under the influence of Medical Marijuana and claimed to have his Medical Marijuana Application paperwork at home in Denver. Two green pill bottles containing marijuana were recovered from the vehicle.

Case # 2010-167   Dispensary: None

During a vehicle stop the Officer located a bag of marijuana. The driver claimed the marijuana belonged to a friend that is a Medical Marijuana Licensee but would not disclose the individual's name. The Driver also admitted to assisting a friend move Medical Marijuana Plants from a residence involved in a prior drug bust. The prior drug case is Case # 2010-132 and involved Herb's Medicinals.

Case # 2010-350   Dispensary: None

While attempting to stop a vehicle the Driver fled. While in contact with the passenger, a Medical Marijuana Licensee, marijuana was located. The Passenger was charged with obstruction for his actions during the contact.

Case #2010-388   Dispensary: Unknown

Juveniles were contacted in the Berthoud Park area in response to a report of Juveniles smoking marijuana. Upon contact the Officer determined that the Juveniles were under the influence of marijuana and confiscated marijuana from them. According to the Officer "the marijuana in possession of both juveniles was decent in grade and was not compressed. These observations made it overtly obvious that the marijuana both kids possessed were purchased from a medicinal marijuana dispensary or from a person with a MMR license that obtained it from a dispensary. The marijuana was not typical brick packed marijuana of low grade from Mexico."

Case # 2010-450   Dispensary: Unknown

During a motor vehicle accident investigation the Driver admitted to smoking Medical Marijuana and had marijuana in their possession. The Driver claimed to have applied for a Medical Marijuana License but did not have the paperwork in possession. The Driver was also under the influence of alcohol and was arrested for DUI/D.

Case # 2010-462   Dispensary: Unknown

During a vehicle contact Officers discovered marijuana and marijuana paraphernalia. The marijuana was packaged in pill bottles which is commensurate with medical marijuana packaging from area dispensaries at the time. 2 adults and 1 juvenile were issued citations.

Case # 2010-478   Dispensary: Unknown

During a vehicle contact the Driver admitted to the Officer that they had smoked marijuana. Officers located marijuana packaged in a purple pill bottle which is was labeled as "ISS x Blue Dream" which is consistent with medical marijuana packaging from area dispensaries at the time. The Driver was NOT a Medical Marijuana Licensee and stated that they did not want to get a licensee due to it making it harder to get a job. The driver was arrested for DUI/D.

Case # 2010-511   Dispensary: Unknown

During a vehicle contact Officers located Hash and a THC Sucker. The driver was NOT a Medical Marijuana Licensee but a passenger was. The Driver was arrested for DUI/D. The Driver's infant daughter was in the vehicle as well as the Driver's juvenile brother and an adult passenger. Social Services was notified.

Case #2010-580 & 2011-187   Dispensary: None

While assisting the FBI with a search warrant for child pornography a 94 plant marijuana grow was located in the garage. A large amount of processed marijuana was also found in the house. When interviewed the subject stated that he was growing the marijuana with the intent to go "Dispensary hopping" to sell the marijuana to dispensaries. The same individual later stole a vehicle and fled the area, robbed a Wal-Mart and led several agencies on high speed chases until finally captured. The individual later stated that he was worried about the then pending local and federal charges. The individual was convicted of manufacturing marijuana with intent to distribute and was also federally indicted. The individual was NOT a Medical Marijuana Licensee.

Case # 2011-144   Dispensary: Colorado Cana Care

While on Patrol the Officer was flagged down by a business owner who stated that the people renting the warehouse adjoining theirs was growing medical marijuana. Upon investigation by the Officer it was determined that the individual renting the space was growing medical marijuana for Colorado Cana Care in violation of the moratorium enacted by the Town of Berthoud Town Council. The grow was removed and the occupants evicted.

Colorado Cana Care is now closed in as the City of Loveland has opted to not allow Dispensaries.

Case# 2011-165   Dispensary: Unknown

Juveniles were contacted at the Berthoud High School under the influence of marijuana. One of the students had marijuana on his person in a pill bottle that was packaged commensurate with medical marijuana packaging from dispensaries at the time. The student admitted to using marijuana to deal with his mental problems.

Case# 2011-301   Dispensary: Unknown

During a suspicious vehicle contact juveniles were located in the vehicle and admitted to smoking marijuana. The marijuana located in the vehicle was packaged in a pill bottle consistent with medical marijuana packaging from area dispensaries at the time.

Case # 2011-363   Dispensary: Unknown

During a suspicious vehicle contact the Driver was arrested for DUI. During the contact the Officer located marijuana packaged in a plastic jar consistent with medical marijuana packaging from area dispensaries at the time. The Driver was NOT a Medical Marijuana Licensee. The passenger was NOT a Medical Marijuana Licensee.

Case # 2011-547   Dispensary: Unknown

During a vehicle stop the Driver was arrested for DUI. During the contact the Driver was found to be in possession of marijuana and marijuana concentrate in a purple pill bottle consistent with medical marijuana packaging from area dispensaries at the time. The Driver also admitted to smoking Hashish and claimed to be a Medical Marijuana Licensee.

Case # 2011-595   Dispensary: Unknown

During a vehicle contact a bag containing 15 grams of marijuana was located. The passenger claimed to be a Medical Marijuana Licensee but stated that it had expired in September 2010. The driver admitted to smoking marijuana earlier and was NOT a Medical Marijuana Licensee.

Case # 12-48   Dispensary: Unknown

During an accident investigation the Officer located marijuana and marijuana paraphernalia. When the Driver asked about it stated that they were his and that he was a Medical Marijuana Licensee but stated that his license had expired. The Driver was arrested for DUI. The marijuana in the plastic container was packaged consistent with medical marijuana packaging from area dispensaries at the time. The Driver had his juvenile children in the vehicle with him at the time of the accident.

Case #12-75   Dispensary: Unknown

During a child abuse investigation it was noted by the Officer that the child indicated that the parents were marijuana smokers and that they smoke in the house. The father and mother both admitted to smoking marijuana and being Medical Marijuana Licensees. A referral was made to Social Services.

Case # 12-78   Dispensary: Unknown

During a vehicle contact the Officer located a blue container of marijuana that was packaged consistent with medical marijuana packaging from area dispensaries at the time. The Driver was arrested for DUI/D and was NOT a Medical Marijuana Licensee.

Compiled by:

Officer Jeremy Yachik
Berthoud Police Department

Drug endangered children - are those living in dangerous drug environments because of parents or caregivers who manufacture, cultivate, distribute, and/or abuse illegal substances. Being raised in these environments creates outcomes for children that may include – neglect, physical or emotional abuse, lack of supervision, lack of parenting or nurturing role models, poor nutrition, deprivation and unsanitary living conditions.

ENDNOTES

Preface:

1. News Fix, posted by Jon Brooks, RAND Study: LA Crime Increased When Pot Dispensaries Closed; City Attorney Says Data 'Deeply Flawed', ***http:// blogs.kqed.org/newsfix/2011/09/21/rand-study-la-crime-increased-when-pot-dispensaries-close-city-attorney-says-data-deeply-flawed/***, accessed March 16, 2012
2. StopTheDrugWar.com, No evidence Medical Marijuana Dispensaries Cause Crime, RAND Study finds, by Philip Smith, October 3, 2011 (issue #703), *http://stopthedrugwar.org/chronicle/2011/oct/03/no_evidence_ medical_marijuana_di*, accessed March 16, 2012

Chapter 2:

1. 2011 World Drug Report, *http://www.unodc.org/documents/ data-and-analysis/WDR2011/World_Drug_Report_2011_ebook.pdf*, accessed March 15, 2012
2. U.S. News Health, Pot Use Could Double Risk of Car Crash, Research Shows, By Steven Reinberg, *HealthDay Reporter, http://health.usnews. com/health-news/news/articles/2012/02/10/pot-use-could-double-risk-of-car-crash-research-shows,* accessed March 15, 2012
3. MARIJUANA: The greatest cause of illegal drug abuse, Office of National Drug Control Policy Executive Office of the President Washington, DC 20503 July 2008, *http://www.justice.gov/dea/statistics/Marijuana_2008. pdf*, accessed March 15, 2012
4. U.S. Drug Enforcement Administration, *http://www.justice.gov/dea/2010_ successes.html*, accessed March 15, 2012
5. William J. Bennett, a CNN contributor, is the author of *The Book of Man: Readings on the Path to Manhood.* He was U.S. secretary of education from 1985 to 1988 and director of the Office of National Drug Control

Policy under President George H.W. Bush, *http://www.thomasnelson.
com/the-book-of-man.html*

6. Gabriel G. Nahas, MD, PhD, a research professor of anesthesiology at
    the College of Physicians and Surgeons at Columbia University in New
    York City, who has written 400 scientific articles, interview by LISTEN,
    Journal of Better Living.

Chapter 3:

> "There is evidence to show that a 'zero tolerance' approach to
> policing is more effective:"

1. *The Sunday Times*, 8 July 2001
2. *Drug misuse declared in 2000: results from the British Crime Survey*, *Op
    cit*, Table 2.1, page 13
3. *Daily Mail*, 15 February 2002
4. CompStat Citywide Year Historical Comparison 2001 through 1993,
    Police Department City of New York see *http://www.nyc.gov/html/nypd/
    html/pct/cspdf.html* as at 8 April 2002
5. *The Herald*, 3 April 2002 *http://www.christian.org.uk/html-publications/
    cannabis.htm*, accessed March 22, 2012

Chapter 4:

1. Alcoholism—SAMHSA Health Information Network
2. Dr. Robert DuPont, former director of NIDA Community, April 20, 2010,
    commentary
3. American Lung Association, February 2010 Report
4. University of Michigan Study, 2010 for NIDA
5. 2010 National Drug Threat Assessment
6. National Highway Traffic Safety Administration, 2008
7. ONDCP Director Gil Kerlikowske Statement, March 4, 2010
8. National Drug Control Strategy, February 2007
9. Treatment Episode Data Set Highlights, 2009, SAMHSA
10. (Prolong effects after smoking marijuana-driving and flashbacks)
    Cannabis—Hash and Marijuana—A factsheet from the Swedish Council
    for Information on Alcohol and other drugs, seeas at 19 March 2002.
    See also Hollister, L E, 'Health Aspects of Cannabis', Pharmacological
    Reviews, 38(1), 1986, page 7; Ashton, C H, 'Ad http://www.can.se/

showStandard.asp?id=27verse effects of cannabis and cannabinoids', Op cit, pages 637-649

11. Flashbacks with marijuana use, See www.drugscope.org.uk/ druginformation/drugsearch/ds_results.asp?file=\wip\11\1\1\flashbacks. htm as at 19 March 2002

12. Thousands of Colo. marijuana applications on hold, *Denver Post, http:// www.denverpost.com/news/marijuana/ci_19509992?IADID=Search- www.denverpost.com-www.denverpost.com#ixzz1pyzKIKVZ,* accessed March 23, 2012

13. Larimer County Sheriff's Office press release received from *Sheriff-Press-Release [sheriff-press-release@co.larimer.co.us]*, March 23, 2012

Chapter 5:

1. U.S. Attorney General, District of Colorado, John Walsh memo to Colorado Attorney General, John Suthers, April 26, 2011, *http://www. concernedfccitizens.org/images/stories/US%20Atty%20Walsh%20 Letter%20Med%20MJ.pdf*, accessed March 14, 2012

2. MEMORANDUM FOR UNITED STATES ATTORNEYS, FROM: James M. Cole Deputy Attorney General, June 29, 2011, *http://www. concernedfccitizens.org/images/stories/Cole%20Memo.pdf*, accessed March 14, 2012

3. On August 1, 2011, an attorney, David G. Evans, Esq. from Flemington, New Jersey, legal memorandum online at *http://www.concernedfccitizens. org/images/stories/CSAMEMOAUGUST12011.pdf*, at the time of this publication, accessed March 14, 2012

4. Two more marijuana initiatives filed, *Denver Post, http://www. denverpost.com/breakingnews/ci_20167843/two-more-marijuana- initiatives-filed?IADID=Search-www.denverpost.com-www.denverpost. com#ixzz1q0Xk9nh1*, accessed March 23, 2012

Chapter 8:

1. *American Council for Drug Eduction's, http://www.acde.org/common/ Marijana.htm*

2. DEA, "Speaking Out Against Drug Legalization," 2003 and 2010 (see document for specific citation)

3. SAMHSA, 2009 Annual Survey on Drug Use and Health, September 2010
4. DEA, "DEA Position on Marijuana," July 2010 (see document for specific citations)
5. Bovassco, G., *American Journal of Psychiatry*, 2001
6. Dr. Christian Thurstone, MD, Director, Denver Health—Substance Abuse, Treatment, Education and Prevention Programs
7. SAMHSA, "Highlights for the 2008 Treatment Episode Data Set"
8. SAMHSA, "2009 National Survey of Drug Use and Health," September 2010
9. The research was prepared by the Healthy and Drug Free Colorado, endorsed by the Colorado Drug Investigators Association.
10. *http://healthydrugfreecolorado.org/default.aspx/MenuItemID/170/MenuGroup/Home.htm*
11. Dr. Christian Thurstone, a psychiatrist with board certifications in addiction treatment and child and adolescent care, February 1, 20120, Denver Westword Blogs, Medical marijuana fallout: Kids getting addicted to their "medicine," psychiatrist says, *http://blogs.westword.com/latestword/2010/02/medical_marijuana_fallout_heal.php*, accessed March 26, 2012

Chapter 10:

1. SAMHSA, "2009 National Survey of Drug Use and Health," September 2010
2. CNOA, "The Myths of Drug Legalization," 1994
3. Cesar Analysis of 2009 National Highway Transportation and Safety Administration FARS Data
4. Cramer and Associates, "Study Shows Passage of California Cannabis Initiative Will Increase Traffic Deaths"
5. "Drugged Driving Getting Worse in Colorado," 9News.com, 2011 February 17
6. National Highway Traffic Safety Administration Report, 2009
7. Concerned Citizens for Drug Prevention, Inc. citing National Transportation and Safety Board, 1994
8. French National Institute for Transport and Safety Research, published December. 3, 2005, issue of the British Medical Journal, *http://www.bmj.com/content/331/7529/1371.full*, accessed March 22, 2012

9. Read more about Dr. DuPont's interview: *http://www.pbs.org/wgbh/pages/ frontline/shows/drugs/interviews/dupont.html#ixzz1pVfL5bXZ*,   accessed March 18, 2012
10. *http://seattletimes.nwsource.com/avantgo/2017782727.html*,   accessed March 18, 2012

Chapter 11:

1. DEA, "Speaking Out Against Drug Legalization," 2003 and 2010 (see document for specific citation)
2. U.S. Department of Health and Human Services, "Marijuana—April 26"
3. National Drug-Free Workplace Alliance, September 21, 2010
4. InsuranceQuotes.com, Health insurance coverage for medical marijuana? No way, dude!, by Brittany Hutson and John Egan, *http://www. insurancequotes.com/health-insurance-medical-marijuana/*,   accessed March 19, 2012

Chapter 12:

1. DEA, "Speaking Out Against Drug Legalization," 2003 and 2010 (see document for specific citation)
2. ONDCP, "New Report Finds Higher Levels of THC in U.S. Marijuana to Date," May 2009
3. *Los Angeles Times* | Health, Marijuana more potent than ever, June 12, 2008, by Janet Cromley, *http://latimesblogs.latimes.com/booster_ shots/2008/06/marijuana-more.html*, accessed March 22, 2012

Chapter 13:

1. DEA, "Speaking Out Against Drug Legalization," 2003 and 2010 (see document for specific citation)
2. SAMHSA, 2009 Annual Survey on Drug Use and Health, September 2010
3. DEA, "DEA Position on Marijuana," July 2010 (see document for specific citations)
4. Bovassco, G., *American Journal of Psychiatry*, 2001
5. Dr. Christian Thurstone, MD, Director, Denver Health—Substance Abuse, Treatment, Education and Prevention Programs
6. SAMHSA, "Highlights for the 2008 Treatment Episode Data Set"

7. SAMHSA, "2009 National Survey of Drug Use and Health," September 2010

8. CNOA, "The Myths of Drug Legalization," 1994

9. Cesar Analysis of 2009 National Highway Transportation and Safety Administration FARS Data

10. Cramer and Associates, "Study Shows Passage of California Cannabis Initiative Will Increase Traffic Deaths"

11. "Drugged Driving Getting Worse in Colorado," 9News.com, 2011 February 17

12. National Highway Traffic Safety Administration Report, 2009

13. Concerned Citizens for Drug Prevention, Inc. citing National Transportation and Safety Board, 1994

14. U.S. Department of Health and Human Services, "Marijuana—April 26"

15. National Drug-Free Workplace Alliance, September 21, 2010

16. ONDCP, "New Report Finds Higher Levels of THC in U.S. Marijuana to Date," May 2009

17. National Institute of Drug Abuse, "Marijuana," 2010

18. ONDCP, Director Kerlikowske Speech, March 4, 2010

19. ONDCP, "Marijuana: Know the Facts," October 2010

20. Bureau of Justice Assistance Report, "Substance Abuse and Treatment, State and Federal Prisoners," January 1999

21. *Washington File*, U.S. Department of State, 14 March 2000 see *http://usinformation.state.gov/topical/global/drugs/monsen.htm* as at 10 April 2002, quote of President Bill Clinton's head of drug policy

22. FoxNews.com, Smoking one joint is equivalent to 20 cigarettes, Study Says, published January 29, 2008, *http://www.foxnews.com/story/0,2933,326309,00.html#ixzz1pX46G2m4*, accessed March 18, 2012

23. UCLA study comparing the impact of tobacco cigarettes to marijuana consumption, Coloradoan, by Bruce Blackwell, Gannett News Service, New York, December 7, 1978

24. Journal of the AAPN, Vol. 1, No. 1, 1976, "Chronic Effects of Cannabis"

25. *Denver Post*, Posted: 01/31/2010 01:00:00 AM MST, Updated: 02/01/2010 02:11:14 PM MST, Opinion Letter by Dr. Thurstone, *Smoke and mirrors: Colorado teenagers and marijuana—Denver Post http://www.denverpost.com/opinion/ci_14289807#ixzz1qFFpZmTm*, accessed March 26, 2012

Chapter 14:

1. Proclamation for Colorado's public health and safety, we are opposed to legalizing marijuana for recreational use: *http://healthydrugfreecolorado. org/default.aspx/MenuItemID/181/MenuSubID/31/MenuGroup/Home.htm*

Chapter 15:

1. From News Weekly, March 8 2003, By Richard Egan, Marijuana may be causing deaths, *http://www.katinkahesselink.net/health/canabis.html*, accessed March 22, 2012

2. The Telegraph. "Cannabis use causes 'hundreds of deaths a year', coroner warns" February 2003, *http://alcoholism.about.com/b/a/039646.htm*, and *http://www.allaboutworldview.org/human-suffering.htm*, accessed March 22, 2012

3. Substance Abuse and Mental Health Services Administration, Mortality Data from the Drug Abuse Warning Network, 2001 (PDF), January 2003, see http://dawninformation.samhsa.gov/old_dawn/pubs_94_02/mepubs/ files/ DAWN2001/DAWN2001.pdf.

Other sources used throughout the book:

Top ten reasons not to legalize marijuana, Healthy and Drug Free Colorado, Colorado Drug Investigators Association, www.healthydrugfreecolorado. org *http://gallery.mailchimp.com/a538961424b00a635442bb363/files/ Top_10_Reasons_Not_to_Legalize_Marijuana_Colorado_1_.pdf*

Director Thomas J. Gorman, Rocky Mountain High Intensity Drug Trafficking Area, *http://healthydrugfreecolorado.org/default.aspx/MenuItemID/170/ MenuSubID/29/MenuGroup/Home.htm*, accessed March 14, 2012

Medical Marijuana Distribution Centers, Questions & Answers, *http:// healthydrugfreecolorado.org/default.aspx/MenuItemID/170/ MenuSubID/41/MenuGroup/Home.htm*, accessed March 14, 2012

Ray Martinez has published eight books; the latest books are:

Baby Boy-R: *A memoir about Ray Martinez finding his biological mother only to discover she was a victim and thought he had died—yet finding other siblings he never knew.*
ISBN 978-0-595-44746-6

Just Another Opinion: *A collection of short stories on issues ranging from national to local issues; a second sequel to Saturday's Opinion book*
ISBN 978-0-9644652-8-2

From Darkness to Light; the Mai Tran journey of passion: *A true story of a 15-year-old boy's escape from Vietnam as one of the boat people in the '70s*
ISBN 978-0-9644652-6-8

BOOKS THAT RAY MARTINEZ HAS BEEN INCLUDED IN

The Death MERCHANT, by Joseph C. Goulden
ISBN 0-671-49341-8

Manhunt, The incredible pursuit of CIA Agent Turned Terrorist, by Peter Maas
ISBN 0-394-55293-8

101 Memorable Men of Northern Colorado, by Arlene Ahlbrandt
ISBN 0-9663932-8-7

Modern visions along the Poudre Valley, by Phil Walker
ISBN 1-887982-13-2

Hit from behind . . . out of perfect timing came perfect chaos . . . by Jim Heckel
ISBN 978-1-60791-034-3

50 Interviews—Dream It, Live It, Love It, by Don McGrath.
ISBN 978-0-98229-071-2

The Blueprint; how the democrats won Colorado, by Adam Schrager and Rob Witwer, ISBN 978-1-936218-00-4

Mom; a celebration of mothers from storycorps, by Dave Isay,
ISBN 978-1-59420-261-2

INDEX

medical marijuana dispensaries
(MMD), 9, 11, 37, 105, 111,
181
impact of, 39
pros and cons of banning, 43–44
regulation of, 42
Medicinal Gardens of Colorado, Inc.,
78
Montante, Joseph, 47–48
Morris, Luke, 163–64

N

Nahas, Gabriel G., 23, 25, 196
National Geographic, 12, 16, 145,
152, 184

O

Office of National Drug Control
Policy, 24–25, 143, 195
Ogden, David, 69
Ogden Memo, 68–69, 94–95
Ohlsen, Kelley, 73

P

Partnership for a Drug-Free
America, 24
Patella, James, 58, 60, 71
Patella, Nancy, 15, 58, 60, 71
Patzer v. Loveland, 84
People v. Shell, 83
People v. Watkins, 81
Poudre School District, 15–16, 98,
106–7, 112–13
pro-drug movement. *See* drug
legalization movement

R

Rand Corporation, 11
Rathke v. MacFarlane, 80
Reagan, Nancy, 186
Reinhardt, Neil C., 156, 158
Rocky Mountain High-Intensity
Drug-Trafficking Area, 26
Rogers, Chris, 149
Ryan (e-mail sender), 165

S

Sarah (e-mail sender), 164
Sawyer, Ginny, 56
Scramstad, Kirk, 49
Smith, Justin, 17, 78, 100
Smith, Nancy, 16, 63–64, 74
snake oil, 4, 12
Special Investigations Unit (SIU), 10
Spitzer, Ray, 180, 183
Steve (e-mail sender), 150
Suthers, John, 45, 66, 77, 138, 197

T

Tammy (e-mail sender), 154
Task Force on Marijuana
Dispensaries, 11
tetrahydrocannabinol (THC), 171,
173–74, 181, 183–84, 187
Thurstone, Christian, 108, 110, 114,
133–34, 198–99
Titus Andronicus, 152
Troxell, Wade, 18, 73, 93, 104
Troy (e-mail sender), 151
Turner, Hamish, 143

V

victims, drug-use, 28
Volkow, Nora, 127

W

Walsh, John F., 66
Williams, Dallas, 47–48
Wilson, Jerry, 15, 112

Y

Yachik, Jeremy, 185
Young, Dillon, 166

Z

Zoetewey, Debbie, 89

Edwards Brothers Malloy
Thorofare, NJ USA
May 31, 2012